THE LADDER
OF LIFE

THE LADDER OF LIFE

BALANCING THE CLIMB

Stuart Symington

Published by Quickfox Publishing,
PO Box 50660 West Beach 7449
Cape Town, South Africa
www.quickfox.co.za | info@quickfox.co.za

The Ladder of Life: Balancing the Climb
ISBN 978-0-620-94577-6

First edition 2021

Copyright © 2021 WordPowerOnline.com (Pty) Ltd
www.wordpoweronline.com

All rights reserved.
No part of this publication may be reproduced, stored in a retrieval system, or transmitted, in any form or by any means, without the prior written permission of the author: stusymo@gmail.com

Editor: Michelle Bovey-Wood
Cover and book designer: Vanessa Wilson
Typesetting and production: Quickfox Publishing
Printed by: Digital Action SA, Cape Town, South Africa

DEDICATION

I am forever grateful to my parents for giving me life; to my children, siblings, friends and work colleagues for giving meaning to my life; and to my wife for giving me unconditional love in this life. Gaily, you have been the wind at my back.

My relationship with my children is the best investment that I could ever have made over the years. I can only marvel at life's generous interest on that investment, including the six, healthy grandchildren with whom I have been blessed so far.

For this reason, I dedicate this book to my grandchildren, and any other grandchildren who have plans to join us at a later stage.

Finally, I offer my heartfelt thanks to all of those authors whom I have either quoted in the coming pages, or listed at the end of the book. You have given me hundreds of hours of reading pleasure. I do hope that I have done sufficient justice to your thoughts that are knitted together here with mine.

CONTENTS

Introduction 11
Letter to my Sons 13

1. **THE MAGIC OF SEEING THE BIGGER PICTURE** 17
   The covert curriculum 18
   What is a successful life? 19
   Bookends of life 24
   The power of choice 27
   Visualisation techniques 32
   The philosophy of karma 38
   Finding the truth 43

2. **EDUCATION, EDUCATION AND EDUCATION** 47
   Our most valuable asset 48
   Welcome to 4th industrial revolution (4IR) 49
   Knowledge decay 50
   The four cornerstones of education 53
   Learning about learning 56

3. **MONEY MATTERS** 59
   Myth 1 60
   Myth 2 60

Working the system 61
Playing by the rules 63
10% of all we earn is ours to keep 65
Investor or speculator? 68
Property prospects 71
Personal financial housekeeping 76

4. EMOTIONAL COMPETENCE: OUR NUMBER
   ONE LIFESKILL 79
   A people's world 80
   Recurring blindspots 82
   Two ears and one mouth 84
   Biting our tongues 85
   The bane of know-it-alls 87
   Sorry really is the hardest word 88
   Trumped by technology 90
   A tactical response to emotional hijacking 91

5. ATTRACTING THE LOVE WE DESERVE 99
   The naivety of youth 100
   Trappings of young love 101
   Choosing a lifelong partner 108
   For the love of marriage 115
   Conscious uncoupling 119
   Polished in the tumbler 122

6. SUPER CHILDREN, SUPER PARENTS 129
   Breaking the mould 130
   A job for life 131
   The crux of parenting 134
   The gift of self-esteem 138

CONTENTS

The emotional credit system 140
Raising the mirror 143
Choice of schooling 150
Afterthoughts on parenting 153

7. DONNING OUR SPIRITUAL ARMOUR 157
   Religious beginnings 158
   Chance discovery 161
   Stilling the mind 164
   Behind the veil 170
   Our one and only certainty 175
   Enlightened leadership 184

Reading list 191

INTRODUCTION

If you have ever wondered whether this life is not all that it's cracked up to be, take heart. This book is designed to tease your curiosity a little further in this regard. Finding a greater sense of purpose and contentment in this life is crucial in being able to look back with infinitely more satisfaction, and far fewer regrets.

In hindsight, there is much that our schools and universities did not teach us that would have been good to know. So, the overarching goal of this book is to offer the reader some insights into this 'hidden curriculum' of life – the stuff we have to find out for ourselves from the School of Hard Knocks.

As we climb the ladder of life, we may encounter some loose rungs or even one or two missing ones. At times we may even feel that our ladder is leaning up against the wrong wall. Safely navigating our way up life's ladder is both an art and a science. The chapters that follow are written with 'the big decisions' in mind – decisions that, made wisely, can change the trajectory of our lives for the better, forever.

This book also contains a myriad of underlying themes that are simple to understand, but not that simple to put into practice. Herein lies the challenge for us all: to ring the changes, and then to live those changes in our lives.

Some of the underlying themes in this book include:

- Breaking the mould of our upbringing, despite the very best efforts and intentions of those who brought us up;
- Looking at the bigger picture that life has to offer, and tackling, with a sense of urgency and zest, the opportunities that present themselves;
- Getting to know ourselves really well so that we can become our own best friend, and the very best version of who we want to be;
- Seeking a balance amongst the six most important areas of our lives: our health; wealth; family; friends; livelihood and spirituality;
- Disengaging from going through life on 'autopilot', and switching to 'manual' instead, so that we can take charge of our own destinies; and
- Taking leaves out of the books of those wise souls who made a mega-difference while walking this planet.

As we grow older and the sands of time flow ever faster, we come to appreciate that every day is a bonus. My hope is that this book motivates you to take life's offerings with both hands and to live each day mindfully, and to the full.

LETTER TO MY SONS

The Autumn of my Life

Dear Andrew and Dean

You might recall that I spoke fondly of your great grandmother, Gags, whom you unfortunately never met.

Every Sunday, from the age of seven, Gags would fetch me from boarding school in her swish Jaguar and whisk me off for the day. Back at her apartment, which was littered with precious antiques, I found refuge in a huge armchair that nearly swallowed me whole every time I clambered into it. The day routinely started with me washing back a few freshly-baked cookies with a glass of chocolate milk. Gags would then slide a footstool under my feet, throw a blanket over my lap, and allow me to quietly unwind after another tough week at school.

Gags was always extremely interested in my life. She would patiently sit there, trying to establish what had happened to me during my school week, but getting a shy, young boy like me to talk about my school activities was like trying to squeeze blood from a stone. I preferred to just sit there pondering the magnitude of life. With great diplomacy, Gags would then offer me a penny for my thoughts. I recall being amused by that saying which, even back then, seemed rather old-fashioned. But it struck a chord in me, and encouraged me to share with her the very privileged school life that she and my grandfather had afforded me. I think that turned out to be therapeutic for both of us.

Your great-grandmother was my great mentor in this life. Strongly influenced by her parents, who were from the Victorian era, she could have been considered a very prim and proper lady. Although she was strict, I never feared her, as she was always concerned with my wellbeing. She believed in me, instilled confidence in me, and was quick to encourage me to play to my strengths. She was also a great proponent of mind over matter. How powerful that attitude was in influencing my life.

You both would have loved Gags and what she stood for. This is why I had no hesitation in using her as a role model in how to raise you both.

Gags came into my life early, and sadly, left early. When I stood there, looking at her motionless body, it felt as if all the air had been sucked out of the room. Sogyal Rinpoche was right: "Death is a mirror in which the whole meaning of life is reflected."

The School of Hard Knocks had dealt me the cruellest of blows early on in my journey, and it was only over time – being the great healer that it is – that I began to understand and appreciate the extent to which my formative years with Gags had moulded the rest of my life. Soren Kierkegaard insightfully remarked: "Life is lived forwards but only understood backwards."

I can hear Gags again now, nearly 40 years later, offering me a penny for my thoughts. Instead of asking me to tell her about my school life, she seems to be asking me to tell others about the school of life. I don't feel particularly qualified to do this, but I think I have had an eventful life. On reflection, it does seem a dreadful waste to let learnings of a lifetime go to the grave without making them available to subsequent generations.

Historian George Santayana, said: "Those who cannot remember the past are condemned to repeat it." So, my humble offering here is left to you and your offspring, but only if it should interest you.

In case you decide not to read any further than this letter, I wish to leave just two thoughts here with you:

Since you are both scientists, I will approach the first topic with delicate caution. I feel strongly that there is a spiritual void that is rendering too many people's lives meaningless today. The eternal chase for material gain seems to dominate everywhere. Yet, the pursuit of it is no more futile than "trying to find a black cat in a dark room", to use a Confucian saying. Excessive materialism brings little sustainable happiness or meaning to our lives, and you can't take it with you when you breathe your last. Have you ever seen a hearse pulling a trailer? Unbeknown to many, giving of yourself to others – rather than taking as much as you can for yourself – is where you can draw most of your contentment in this life.

The second void is the absence of decent parenting. Far too many children have their formative years substantially compromised by parents who skimp on the most important job of their lives. Those families, societies and countries that don't invest in their children, don't invest in their future. I believe that the current bleak state of global affairs partly reflects this inconvenient truth. That is why I have dedicated a chapter to the vital topic of parenting. If one day you are blessed with children of your own, please make the very most of that privileged opportunity to leave this world a better place. It shouldn't be difficult for you, because I am convinced that you will both make fabulous fathers.

Before I forget: a thousand thanks to you both for making me a super-proud dad. Right from the days on which you were both born, you have given me endless joy. Look where you are today. What a tremendous honour it is being your dad!

When I'm six feet under and pushing up the daisies, remember only this: there were simply not enough stars in the night sky to write and tell you both how much I loved you.

Dad xx

P.S. Don't forget the password: 'lego'.

1

THE MAGIC OF SEEING THE BIGGER PICTURE

The covert curriculum

In my early 30s, I read a book that changed my life. It was called *The Magic of Thinking Big*[1] by David Schwartz. It was my first glimpse into the hidden curriculum of life that I affectionately refer to as 'the art of living' – things that most people are only exposed to via the School of Hard Knocks.

Up until that point, the deceit for me had been believing that having banked my degree in my 20s, I was licensed to chase my dreams, line my pockets and set myself up for life. It was naïve of me to believe that, but in the absence of anything that might have led me to conclude otherwise, it was all I had to go by.

So, it was only after picking up Schwartz's book, followed by a raft of other self-help books, that I started to understand all on which I had been missing out. That library of personal development books became my treasure trove that contained the secrets of how to lead a happier, healthier and more rewarding – dare I say more successful – life. Those books provided me with a formula for living that was inspiring, exciting and results-driven. They rammed home the point that it's not only our qualifications that determine what we can achieve in our lives. It is also a combination of *visualising* and *believing* in what we can attain that will successfully take us over the finishing line in most of our endeavours. These two words have magic in them, and they are the keys to unlocking a far greater world than we could ever imagine possible for ourselves.

---

1 Schwartz, D.J. *The Magic of Thinking Big*, Vermilion, 1959.

> *It is not just our aptitude but our attitude that determines our altitude in this life.*

The goal of this book is to offer a sneak preview into life's covert curriculum. It is structured to cover some of life's biggest decisions with which we will be confronted – decisions for which most of us need to be better informed than the education offered by traditional upbringings. The choices that we make in our 20s and 30s have an enormous impact on the rest of our lives. In fact, the quality of those decisions strongly influence whether we will lead a life of significance, or a life of struggle.

The topics covered in this book also deliberately cover those areas of our lives that are renowned for throwing out the toughest challenges. These include appreciating the value of the bigger picture in life; educating ourselves for our chosen vocation; making, managing and multiplying our money; getting along well with others; choosing a suitable life partner; raising children; and addressing our spirituality – including coming to terms with our one and only certainty in this life.

What is a successful life?

Perhaps this is an important concept to clarify upfront, as the term "successful life" is pregnant with subjectivity. Broadly speaking, I believe that a successful life is about achieving the goals that we have set for ourselves. However, this makes the assumption that we have, in fact, set goals. Without these goals, it's not only difficult to know where we are going, but it's also impossible to measure if we're making any progress.

In narrowing down my definition of success a little further, one could say it is about achieving a balanced scorecard over

THE LADDER OF LIFE: BALANCING THE CLIMB

the more important areas of life: our health; wealth; livelihood; family; friends; and spiritual wellbeing. I put health first, because without that, we have precious little else.

At a foundational level, success is about being your own best friend: knowing yourself, liking yourself, caring for yourself and being at peace with yourself. Above all, it is knowing how to motivate yourself, as and when needed, to achieve whatever it is that you have set your heart on.

I started my career as a high school maths teacher because that's what I really wanted to be. Back then, teaching was an extremely demanding job, and no doubt, it still is. As teachers, we used to eat, sleep and breathe teaching and had little time for anything else.

I enjoyed four holidays a year, but had no money to do anything with them because the profession did not pay well. I socialised almost exclusively with teachers, and the conversation always seemed to gravitate towards school matters, staff room politics and the more troublesome students.

After several years of earning a meagre teacher's salary, I was struggling to pay my bills. It was around that time that I picked up and became riveted by my first few self-help books. It was a category of literature to which I had previously been oblivious. To this day, I recall one book in particular: Og Mandino's *University of Success*[2] That book was so inspirational that I immediately hung up my teaching boots and rung the changes in my life.

Back then, that was a really tough call to make. Teaching was the only career I had hankered after in my youth; it was also the only profession for which I had qualified; and it was the only job I had ever known.

---

2 Mandino, O, *University of Success*, Random House, 1994.

20

Fortunately, a friend of mine had produced two videos for commercial consumption. Those videos taught managers how to discipline and dismiss people fairly in the workplace, covering aspects of procedural and substantive fairness in great detail. Since I had absolutely no background knowledge on industrial relations at the time, I essentially had to go back to school. I trawled through those two 45-minute videos with a fine toothcomb and learned every last titbit of information in both of them. I then familiarised myself with the videos' strengths and weaknesses; which companies would want to view them; why they would want to buy them; how to actually sell them and close the deal; how to get additional sales leads; and how to listen for new ideas that could generate new products off the back of those videos.

When I had plucked up enough courage and confidence, I set out in my car into the great unknown with only the shirt on my back. I had to learn the geography of my home town (Cape Town) fast, including the names and types of businesses populating it. Importantly, I had to find the contact details of all potential buyers of those videos within the companies I had identified. I learned the hard way that it was one thing to get an appointment with a buyer, but quite another to get the buyer to sign the deal.

This was all a monumental shock to my system. My parents and many of my friends thought that I was crazy to have left the safety of a salaried job, but at the time, I reckoned nothing ventured, nothing gained. Looking back, it might have been a brave move; but it was actually more of a profound turning point in my life. After that, nothing was ever the same again.

Within a year, I had gone from being an 8am to 4.30pm suburban government employee, to a 7am to all-hours-of-the-night, self-employed, national salesman. In that first year, I sold a pantechnicon-load of videos to companies around the whole country. In so doing, I had broken the mould of my belief system, my education and my upbringing. A brand-new world had opened up to me, and it seemed that even the sky was no longer the limit.

Thrillingly, I was comfortably able to pay my bills.

As Nelson Mandela once famously observed: *"It only seems impossible until you've done it."* That was all of 30 years ago! I now find myself writing to encourage others to also break free from the mental chains that might be binding their thinking and limiting their view on life. It was Jean-Jacques Rousseau who wrote: *"Man is born free but everywhere he is in chains."* However I do think that most of us are largely responsible for putting ourselves in these chains.

I recall, as a very young boy, my father helping me to climb a ladder in the garden so that I could be 'taller' than him. How different he and the garden had seemed from the top of that ladder. When I was a little older and was able to (disobediently, for which I got a hiding) climb on to the roof of our house, what a change in scenery that offered: the neighbours' houses and gardens all suddenly came into full view, offering me a completely different perspective on what I was used to seeing.

When the cable car hauled me to the top of Table Mountain for the very first time, I experienced a breathtaking view of Cape Town. The city sprawled out in front of me and stretched into the distance before disappearing over the horizon. I recall being able to determine more or less where we lived in that concrete jungle. How tiny our neighbourhood had suddenly seemed.

When I experienced my first night flight, I was astonished to see though my window how huge cities that lay 40 000 feet beneath the aeroplane shrank into tiny patches of light surrounded by sheets of black void.

When I picked up my first handful of personal growth books, it was like climbing on to the figurative 'ladder of life'. Just being on the first rung started to give me an aerial view on things – just as I had experienced when I had literally climbed on to the ladders, roofs, cable cars and aeroplanes I have described above. By the time I had reached the second rung of the ladder, the door to the library of life had been flung open.

Certain powerful personal growth books quickly stripped me of my blinkers, and revealed a much bigger picture of life than I had ever imagined possible. There was no looking back after that. It opened up my world to extensive travel, exciting new jobs, fascinating people from all walks of life, money and investment opportunities, as well as endless learning opportunities. It created a vast array of options for me – including the courage and confidence to do things differently from the way I had been brought up to do them.

The moment that it dawned on me that my future lay firmly in my own hands, I was overcome by a sense of urgency to immediately capitalise on that epiphany. Life was there for the taking – but only once I had first realised it, and then acted on it.

It is my greatest wish that this book helps you to find and rapidly take that first step on to the ladder of life. I hope that it ignites within you all sorts of possibilities for reinventing yourself and finding the 'real you' – the best possible version of who you can be. If it just stirs your thinking and encourages you to try new things in different ways, thereby forever changing the course of your life for the better, writing this book will have been well worth it.

Perhaps this is an opportune moment to recall the words of Albert Einstein: *"The definition of insanity is doing the same thing over and over again, but expecting different results."*

The remaining part of this chapter is designed to stretch

your thinking to see the bigger picture of life: to exercise your power of choice and convert your thoughts into action; to adopt visualisation techniques to improve your decision-making skills; to onboard the philosophy of karma and create positive outcomes for yourself; and to engage in truth-finding so that you can plot your way towards a better quality of life.

Bookends of life

Imagine peeking through the eyepiece of the Hubble Telescope that's orbiting space, and being able to see the latest and greatest developments in the far reaches of the universe. Worlds beyond our imagination are continuously evolving out there.

Now imagine peering through the eyepiece of an electron microscope to see the detailed structure of an individual cell, and all that the nanoworld has to offer. It may not be visible to the naked eye, but it's a world that has a deep impact on us at a cellular level, and consequently on our lives. Just think of the COVID-19 virus as an example.

Now, let's for a moment consider that these two visual extremes are, for all intents and purposes, the bookends of life. Everything that lies between these two worlds is what is on offer to us. Fascinatingly, these bookends are being shifted further and further apart as we discover more and more knowledge about this world in which we live. What's more, the internet brings much of this knowledge right into the comfort of our own homes. We have Google, YouTube and many other electronic encyclopaedias of the universe at our fingertips.

Consider, too, that if we include the history of all that has gone before us, the picture expands even further. If we take into account the world that lies just beyond what the conscious mind can perceive (more about that in a later chapter), we are immediately humbled by just how unfathomable this bigger picture really is, and what it can potentially offer us.

Now imagine getting a call from Space-X, offering you a once-in-a-lifetime opportunity to travel to the moon and back. If you had the courage to don your galactical glasses and board their spaceship, you would experience first-hand how no one sees the bigger picture quite like an astronaut. You would most likely share the same sentiment that James Lovell did from Apollo 8 back in 1968. When Lovell looked out through his space capsule's window, he saw Spaceship Earth floating like a blue marble in space. He held up his thumb and stated that he could hide behind his thumbnail an object that held five billion people – including everything that he had ever known in his whole life. What an extraordinarily privileged perspective that was!

That well-documented space-to-Earth perspective is called the 'overview effect'. It occurs when astronauts encounter a profound cognitive shift in their own awareness of who they are and their role in this world. Lovell, himself, testified to that out-of-Earth experience by saying that when he "saw the Earth like this from 240 000 miles away, the reality of his world suddenly seemed to expand to infinity". He began to question his very own existence, including how he fitted into the picture of what he saw in front of him. He likened it to God giving mankind a stage on which to perform, but the end was "entirely up to us".[3]

---

3   AARP, Jim Lovell looks back on Nasa Apollo Missions, www.aarp.org/politics-society/history/info-2018/jim-lovell-apollo-nasa.html (Accessed: 20 April 2021)

After gravitating back to Earth from the blue yonder, the Russian cosmonaut, Gennady Padalka, had the following insightful remark to make:

"Earth is unique in its ability to support life as we know it. Astronomy has shown us that we are one amongst billions of worlds in the Milky Way Galaxy. Yet, our tangled web of geology, ecology and biology makes this strange rock the only one in reach that's just right for us humans."[4]

By some serendipitous, cosmological providence, we are lucky to be here. We might be inhabiting a speck of dust somewhere in the backyard of the universe, but we're here. If we take the time to look, listen and learn, we are surrounded by a massive laboratory of opportunities every day of our lives.

Let's be honest

It's time to ask a couple of questions that require brutal honesty:

- Are we making the most of what amounts to an extraordinarily privileged existence that has, by some sheer chance, come our way?
- Do we see the opportunities that surround us for what they are, and to where they can lead?
- Are we jumping out of bed every morning to embrace the opportunities that life throws at us?

---

4 Drake, Nadia, They Saw the Earth from Space. Here's how it changed them, National Geographic, www.nationalgeographic.com/magazine/article/astronauts-space-earth-perspective (Accessed: 20 April 2021)

If you have answered: "No," to the above questions, you're definitely not alone – not by a long chalk. Most people live on autopilot, hoping that life will come to them and somehow work out for the best one day.

If you found reasons why it wasn't possible to answer in the affirmative to any of the above questions – like it's all just too daunting to contemplate – then know this: our minds are brilliant at conjuring up a million and one reasons why we can't do something. A lack of self-belief won't even get us out of the starting blocks. It's easier to say: "No," and make an excuse than it is to say: "Yes," and have to do something about it. For the lazier among us, change requires commitment to a whole lot of effort. But it is in making the effort that we change our lives.

To get around any inertia from which we may be suffering, it might first help to remind ourselves that successfully achieving our goals can only be done one step at a time. In much the same way, a house can only be built one brick at a time. Secondly, we can apply that energising Nike slogan: "Just do it!" It has been shown time and again that by taking action without thinking too much about it, we can experience surprisingly good results. If we do this often enough, our actions can become healthy habits that automatically start to rewire our thinking. Our minds then galvanise our energies into doing the right things, in the right way, to get the right results. It's how the human mind works.

The power of choice

> *The difference between those who act versus those who suffer from inertia boils down to how go-getters approach their lives.*

Go-getters

These are people who seem to subscribe to Norman Vincent Peale's view: *"Shoot for the moon. Even if you miss, you'll land among the stars!"* Go-getters do the following:

- They spend considerable time visualising a bigger picture of what they can do about their future.
- They imagine the best version of who they can become.
- They design a roadmap for their lives and have a clear plan of where they are going, how they are going to get there, and when they will get there.
- They abandon their comfort zones and courageously embrace new ideas, new places, new people and new experiences.
- They chase big dreams and create happiness and wealth for themselves and their families.
- They go in search of the freedom that life offers to those who seek it.

Now, there is some 'great news' and 'not-so-great news' I would like to share with you. Let's start with the not-so-great news. Unfortunately, life doesn't really work out favourably for those who sit back and wait for things to come to them. Those people can wait an exceedingly long time – sometimes their whole lives. It can be likened to watching paint dry on life's wall. Put a little more bluntly: the universe is not really that willing to support those who feel entitled and couldn't be bothered to help themselves.

The great news is that we can grab life by the horns and change our destiny in an instant. All it requires of us is one thing: that we exercise our power of choice. The greatest faculty that mankind possesses is his ability to choose. Everything we end up doing in this life comes down to choices we have made.

Doing nothing – sweet Fanny Adams, in colloquial terms – is also a choice. If we do not exercise any of the options in front of us, by default, we have actually made the choice to do nothing.

Most go-getters will acknowledge that the very moment they realised that they had become prisoners of their own minds was the very same moment that they had planned their escape. It was that 'aha moment' that awakened the sleeping giant within them, allowing them to choose possibilities that changed the course of their lives.

In contrast, if we can't see past the front doors of our own homes, or further than the ends of our desks at work, then we must accept that we're not really going anywhere in our lives. That's absolutely fine if that's all we want. But then we've made a conscious choice to sidestep what life has waiting in the wings for us. If we choose to go this essentially non-eventful route, there's a high probability that we will have precious little to show for it when all is said and done. In this scenario, we are likely to end up bemoaning our fate and regretting the inactions of our past. It's the road that invariably leads to self-pity, which is not a particularly endearing character trait.

Life doesn't have to be like this!

If we need to make a decision to change the direction in which our life is going, then we can make that decision right here and right now.

There's no time like the present to make life-changing decisions. Think about this for a moment: we are what we think. How rosy we want our future to be is entirely a choice we make from the thoughts that we have.

I can already hear some people saying: "He must be joking!

I'm not that talented! My life's done; I've missed the boat!" If we're already saying these kinds of things in our heads, then we're choosing to talk ourselves out of something before we've even started contemplating it.

Schwartz calls this affliction 'excusitis' – a disease that enables people to find every excuse under the sun as to why they can't do something – even if that 'something' is simply making a decision.

> *Every time we choose to sabotage our own minds, we lose yet another opportunity to optimise our potential.*

Each one of us is so much more capable than we realise; yet we have tragically allowed ourselves to think and believe differently.

Know this, too: once we have authentically conceived and chosen who we want to be; what we want to do; where we want to go; and how we're going to get there, two amazing things happen. Firstly, our built-in satellite navigation system goes to work immediately, sending us in the right direction to achieve our goals. Secondly, the energy required to get us there materialises from nowhere. When we are motivated to get up off the couch and to 'go for it', the required energy remarkably seems to appear from nowhere to fuel our efforts – and it's high-octane stuff, too!

Let's take this opportunity to imprint the following three words indelibly onto our memories:

> *Action cures fear!*

We would do well to apply this formula whenever we find ourselves suffering from inertia.

Many people battle to break free from the static mental patterns that have grounded them for years. We can only fly once we see possibilities through a bigger, better and wider-angled lens on life. When we have this perspective, we will attract life-changing prospects into our orbit. After that, there's no looking back.

Let's consider the opposite of big thinking: small thinking, or small-mindedness. The last thing we want to constantly be doing is sweating the small stuff. Richard Carlson covers this beautifully in his book *Don't Sweat the Small Stuff*[5]. People who continually bog themselves down by nit-picking at details, or micro-managing everything and everyone around them are, quite frankly, tiresome to be around. That is not to say that paying attention to life's details isn't important – it is, but it is not essential every minute of every day. It is best not to let the minutiae of life clutter our daily desks and preoccupy our minds. We need to shove that cul-de-sac-thinking to one side, lift our eyes to the horizon, and open up the windows to our minds. There's such a big world out there waiting to blow a fresh new breeze into our thinking. It is up to us to let it in.

If it's time for change, let's make a conscious choice to cut the thinking that has been limiting our progress. Let's yank off that little rear-view mirror that has been focusing our attention on a restricted view of the past. Let's shift our attention to looking through life's wide-angled windscreen instead. The view – and road ahead – is infinitely more interesting, exciting, surprising and rewarding.

---

5 Carlson, R., *Don't Sweat the Small Stuff*, Hachette Books, 1998.

Visualisation techniques

If we want to climb Mount Kilimanjaro, we can literally stand at the foot of the mountain and psych ourselves into scaling the slopes in front of us. Of course, it will require significantly more preparation than that, but at least we will physically be able to see our goal standing in front of us.

> When I was a teenager, I was a high-jumper. I used a technique to psych myself into jumping higher than my mind thought possible: I would sit on the ground and look at the crossbar that was, at times, almost as high as a doorframe. I would visualise myself clearing that height with a few inches to spare. As I stood up, looking constantly at the bar, it seemed to 'drop down' in height from where I had seen it while sitting on the ground. I merely changed the angle at which I viewed the bar, but it was enough for me to Fosbury flop my way into the record books, within a few centimetres of the two-metre mark. Mind over matter is indeed a powerful thing.

More often than not though, it is difficult, even impossible, to see the literal outcome of that for which we are striving. It may be too futuristic, too abstract or too intangible. For example, if our goal is to earn $50K a month as after-tax income, we will need to build a picture in our minds of exactly how we are going to get there. Mind-mapping our way there, visualising the outcome, and then imagining what we can do with that money when we get it, are all motivational tools to bring us closer to achieving our goal.

Here are two visualisation techniques to consider:

Visualisation technique 1: Anticipatory Thinking

There is an unusual, but thought-provoking image that Stephen Covey uses in his must-read book, *The Seven Habits of Highly Effective People*[6].

Covey asks you, the reader, to imagine that you are attending a funeral, and that you are sitting in the front pew of the church.

Upon opening the service sheet, you are startled to discover a picture of yourself on the inside cover of the programme. You are attending your own funeral!

Trying not to show your shock, you immediately turn around to see who has come to pay their respects, and whether you are able to do a headcount. As the preacher starts his sermon, you listen carefully to his words about you. After the last hymn is sung, and the congregants have filed outside, you join them for tea. You meander slowly among the conversations, picking up here and there what they are saying, or not saying, about you. Finally, you leave to contemplate what you saw and heard at your own funeral.

- Did you see everyone you expected to see at your funeral? Or were you disappointed that only a handful of people arrived?
- Were those in attendance miserable that you had passed away? Or were they quite indifferent to your death?

---

6 Covey, S.R., *The Seven Habits of Highly Effective People*, Free Press, 1989.

- Were you happy, perhaps even proud, of what they were saying about you? Or were you deeply disappointed by what you heard?
- Were they sincere about what they were saying? Or could you tell that they were just being polite and saying what was expected of them on such an occasion?

In other words, was there a difference between what you heard and what you would like to have heard? If there was absolutely no difference between the two, you can be delighted. In the eyes of others, you lived the life you had intended.

On the other hand, if there was a big gap between what they said versus what you would have preferred them to have said, then some red lights should be flashing on your radar screen. The bigger the gap, the bigger the opportunity to take stock of your life, and the more repair work you have on your hands. Fortunately, you are still alive, so you can go out there now and correct what you perceive to be your shortcomings.

I think we all know, or certainly have a feeling for, where we are not measuring up in our lives. We ought to have some semblance of understanding of where we can lift our game and how we can do it.

But starting with the end in mind needn't only be about our own demise. We can use the same technique to imagine who we want to become later on in life; what dream job we want to land that will make us feel like we're in seventh heaven; what business we would like to start about which we are super-passionate; the type of person we want to marry; the type of children we want to raise, the dream home we envision building; what marathons around the world we want to run; and the 100 places we want to visit before we take our last breath. The list is endless, and we can fashion it around our own personal desires.

Without a list of goals to chase, achieving any of them will almost certainly remain a pipe dream. Human beings are wired to function in the following way to achieve a goal:

1. We first have to **dream it**, because dreams are the seedlings of reality.
2. We then need to **plan for it**, because those who fail to plan, inadvertently plan to fail.
3. Finally, we need to **actively chase down the goal** to materialise it, otherwise it simply won't happen.

When we repeatedly remind ourselves of the milestones we want to achieve down the line, they lodge themselves in our subconscious. Energy then materialises to fuel our efforts to achieve these milestones. In fact, with enough self-talk about the milestones we're chasing and how we're going to reach them, our minds become gnawingly restless until we get there.

Here's a little tactic to enhance your efforts:
Start by telling others close to you what you're planning to do. There's nothing like subtly 'recruiting' other people to pressure you to get something done. Before long, their interest in your plans will prompt them to intermittently ask you for progress updates. Of course, once you've informed people of your plans, having to tell them later that you have not followed through and delivered on your word is not a position in which you would like to find yourself. If you have enough self-respect and pride in your word being your bond, letting others down is not really an option. This is a great way to put pressure on yourself to come up with the goods. It works!

Life goes by in a flash, and in our later years, the last thing we want to find ourselves saying is: "If only I had just followed through on some of the plans that I had, life would have been so vastly different for me."

Visualisation technique 2: Roadmap Thinking

Roadmaps often look like higgledy-piggledy wiring diagrams. If we know where we want to go, a roadmap will offer us several routes to get there. However, the road that we ultimately choose to take will depend on a raft of factors, including the car we're driving; the state of the roads; the weather conditions on the day; the length of each route; the time of day; and the traffic reports for each road.

Our minds are no different than a roadmap or a wiring diagram. When we make a decision on a major destination we want to reach in our lives, our mind starts plotting ways to get us there. In our mind's eye, we can take ourselves, at the speed of thought, down many different pathways. This is how we 'see' which route is the best one to get us to the destination we have in mind.

In the Netflix series *The Crown*, American President Lyndon Johnson is invited by Her Majesty The Queen to attend a hunting weekend at Balmoral Castle in Scotland. The Queen issued the invitation because at the time, Britain was desperately needing a financial bail-out of £500m, and hobnobbing with Johnson seemed the appropriate ploy to achieve it.

Johnson's advisor suggests to the president that no American president has ever before received such an esteemed invitation – not even John F. Kennedy. It was the swankiest of royal invitations anyone could ever have wished to receive, but instead of being flattered and jumping at the opportunity, Johnson leans back in his chair and ponders the invitation, while speaking his thoughts aloud.

He starts by projecting himself into the future to 'visualise' what he would most likely experience were he to accept the Queen's invitation. He calculates that it would be a long flight across the Atlantic, and an even longer drive to the Scottish castle. He imagines that the castle would be haunted, which would be unappealing to him. He further surmises that he would have to make small talk with people he didn't know and would most likely never meet again. He reminds himself that he has no idea how to hunt, let alone handle a rifle. He would therefore have to learn everything from scratch, and his handicap could even endanger the hunting party. In addition to this, he realises that he would be unable to follow royal protocols. Unlike his predecessors, he would not know which knife or which fork to use for each particular meal served.

Johnson, therefore, declines the invitation, which causes quite a stir on the other side of the Atlantic. No one turns down the Queen.

After thinking through other options at his disposal, Johnson calculates that it would be preferable to entertain the Queen's more charismatic sister, Margaret, who happened to be travelling in the USA at the time. Fortunately, Margaret was able to represent the Crown at the White House. She deputised superbly, and being the socialite that she was, had a whale of a time with Johnson and his presidential partygoers. Not surprisingly, Margaret secured the loan for Britain.

⊰≫∘≪⊱

By first thinking through, or 'mapping', what appeared to be an arduous, unpleasant and potentially dangerous future scenario in his mind, Johnson made the shrewd decision to instead have the party on his own turf. He knew full well that he would have to give Britain the loan anyway, so he determined that he might as well do it on his own terms and turf. It turned out to be a well thought-out decision and a win-win scenario for both countries. After that, the USA took and held the financial upper hand from Britain.

Seeing the bigger picture is about visualising where we want to be, and what we want our lives to look like further down the line. So it is possible, and preferable, to calculate in our mind's eye how we're going to get there, and how we're going to achieve the best possible outcomes for ourselves. Mind-mapping is a technique that should strongly and regularly influence our thinking. Companies do this all the time when strategising the future of their businesses, so why shouldn't we be doing the same for our own lives, too?

Successful people practise futuristic thinking, otherwise called "scenario planning", more commonly than others care to realise. Before we just allow ourselves to blindly accept the status quo and tumbleweed our way through this life, let's rather visualise the options available to us, and then plan and execute exactly which options we want to exercise. We dare not leave it to chance.

> *Remember: Those who struggle to plan their lives, inadvertently plan to struggle in life.*

The philosophy of karma

A well-known Bible verse says: "Whatever a man sows, he will reap in return."[7] This verse can be applied to both our past and our future.

---

[7] NIV, New Testament, Galatians 6:7.

Our personal lives and the situations in which we find ourselves *today*, are usually the direct result of the decisions that we have made (or not made), and the actions that we have taken (or not taken) in the *past*.

If we have worked diligently to improve our quality of life for, say, the last 10 years, then it is likely to manifest in the quality of life that we enjoy today. But this can work the other way round, too, and it can be particularly harsh on those whose past inactions have left them gravely empty-handed today.

To put it bluntly, karma plays itself out as follows:

> *Our current situation is normally the result of our past (in)actions.*

By the same token, the decisions and actions that we take *today* will determine how our *future* pans out. By visualising and planning where we want to be and what we want to be doing when we get there, we set in motion the decisions and actions that we need to take *today*.

If we diligently apply our minds and efforts to our future goals, we will most likely achieve them and enrich our lives in the process. But this one also works the other way: if we have no particular plan for our future, then the chances are high that our situation will not have changed one scrap from when we were pondering our plans years before.

> *Our current (in)actions will determine our future situation.*

Karma is a law of life that is impossible to escape. As soon as we understand the implications of this, we realise the importance of taking the future by the scruff of the neck and becoming the master of our own destinies.

Importantly, this law of karma is particularly powerful when our decisions and their resulting actions impact on others around us. To a large extent, we can determine whether or not we will positively or negatively impact others while on our trajectory to a life worth living. However, every now and then, we will need to pick an alternative path to our goals to avoid harming anyone, including ourselves.

So, the karmic experiences we accrue in our lives can be either positive or negative, and their effect can be felt either immediately, or years later. I have two incidents I would like to share with you. The first demonstrates immediate and positive karmic exchange; and the second reveals delayed karmic retribution.

⊰❦⊱

The first incident occurred late one night after a parliamentary session. A chilly wind was blowing though the deserted city streets as my colleague and I walked back to our cars. Suddenly a young woman emerged from the shadows, clutching her baby. The mother was clearly distressed and begging for enough money for her and her little one to access the city's night shelter.

I stopped, but my colleague walked hurriedly on. I reached for my wallet and pulled out the only note that I had on me at the time: a R100 note! I knew that the shelter wouldn't cost nearly that much for the night, but I reckoned that she and the child needed the money more than I did, so I willingly handed her the money. I will always remember the overwhelming gratitude and relief that lit up her face. That in itself was sufficient reward for me.

The very next day, I had to attend to some business in the north of the country. It was a two-hour flight away from where I lived. While winging my way back that evening, I realised that I had forgotten my wallet at home. That meant that I would be unable to pay for my airport parking ticket and I would not be able to drive myself home. Since my flight was the last one in for the night, spotting a friend or hailing a taxi was out of the question: Plans B and C were scuppered!

I recall just standing there, wondering what on Earth I was going to do next. Then, all of a sudden, out of nowhere, a man in a brown overall came bouncing up to me. He must have been the last porter left on duty. Noticing that I was in a pickle, he asked if he could help me. I told him of my plight, and in a flash he jumped into action. He said that he would fetch his car and take me home. At first, I politely declined his offer, considering it way beyond the call of duty for a porter who was about to knock off from work. But the man insisted.

We jumped into the porter's car and he took me all of the way home, where I quickly ran into my house and fetched my wallet. Then, while we chatted up a storm, he took me all the way back to the airport. Of course I tipped him handsomely when he dropped me off in front of the airport terminal.

While driving home in the wee hours of that morning, it dawned on me that my gesture the night before had been mirrored back to me the very next evening. The universe had determined that one good turn deserved another. That was lightning-quick karma at work!

Some healthy sceptics out there will suggest that what happened was just a lucky coincidence, but others of us will know differently, as we have seen this happen one too many times to simply dismiss it as a coincidence.

> *We attract to ourselves the very energy that we put out to others.*

It helps to be aware of how our decisions impact on the lives of others. Using this awareness to make decisions will, at a minimum, positively affect those around us. In that way, we can avoid attracting any negative karma to ourselves. If we obey this universal principle, we will be pleasantly surprised at how the universe compensates us for this – with interest.

⋘∘⋙

The second incident occurred while I was on business in America. I returned to my New York hotel late one evening to find the FBI and Department of Justice waiting for me in the hotel foyer. Taken by surprise, I was frogmarched to the hotel dining room, where I was subjected to a three-hour interrogation that extended into the early hours of the morning. The officials brandished e-mails and letters that I had written nine years earlier to people in our industry back at home.

To cut a long story short, our country had, many years before, exported products to America, but had paid insufficient respect to America's anti-trust (anti-competitive) laws. This is a criminal offence in America. If you are found guilty, you can go to jail, regardless of whether you are an American citizen or a foreign national.

However, as my letters, in the possession of the FBI, clearly pointed out, I had written to the group of people in my country who were flirting with anti-competitive behaviour and warned them of the potential consequences of their actions. They had ignored my letters, which had been based on solid legal advice at the time. The company I represented subsequently decided to distance itself from those people and their questionable conduct. While the FBI was not fingering me personally, the law enforcement agencies were enquiring how the business had been executed at the time, and who had been behind the anti-competitive business model.

Those back home knew from the start that they were in the wrong. They must have known all along that there was a possibility that the American authorities could catch up with their transgressions – and catch up they did. The culprits got their come-uppance nine years later.

⇜∘⇝

I like to think that there is a cosmic accountant out there who never misses a trick. If we know that what we are doing is against the law, flirting with danger, or bound to affect others negatively, then we should consider choosing another path to avoid the negative consequences that will take root, and eventually reveal themselves. It's just a matter of time.

> *The karmic wheel may sometimes turn a little slower than we'd like, but it does grind very finely.*

The moral of those two illustrations is simple: the decisions we make and the actions that we take will have either positive or negative repercussions down the line – whether they were actions we took yesterday or nine years ago, consequences are inevitable.

Part of seeing the bigger picture in life is appreciating this law of karma. We should use it to create positive outcomes for ourselves, and to always do unto others as we would want done unto ourselves.

Finding the truth

There's nothing worse than making a long-term decision based on incorrect information. It's like punching in the supposed GPS co-ordinates of our destination, only to get there and find that we're in the wrong place! It is crucial to establish fact from fiction before making any far-reaching decisions – especially in a world that is awash with fake news.

⊰≀⊱

I was privileged to be schooled by an extremely wise chairman early on in my business career. One day, he took me aside and asked me to visualise an almighty car accident that had occurred in the centre of a large, busy intersection. That accident was deliberately chosen by my chairman as an analogy for the devastating consequences of the 'big bang' deregulation of our agricultural boards in our country at that time.

He told me to imagine that after the emergency services had taken the injured to hospital and cleared the debris, the investigating officer interviewed bystanders who had witnessed the accident from all four corners of the intersection. After spending considerable time interviewing people and writing up his report, the officer observed something odd: his report was peppered with conflicting opinions from the various witnesses who had seen the same accident. He recalled how each witness had clung ever tighter to their version of events when interrogated further. The officer quietly admitted to himself that some of the witnesses seemed more credible than others. That left him pondering what had really happened on that fateful day.

My chairman then wrapped up his story about the imaginary accident by stating that unfortunately, the investigating officer had no video footage to assist him with his investigation. So, to successfully unravel what had actually happened, and to be worth his salt, he would have to adhere to the following three principles to get to the 'bigger picture' i.e. the truth of what had happened.

1. **Listen to every last witness account.** It was the only way to get to the equivalent of a 'drone view' of what happened. The witnesses' versions sounded contradictory only because they saw the accident from different angles. Just because someone said that they didn't see what someone else saw

does not mean that it didn't happen. It was more likely that their view was simply obstructed or limited.

2. **Stick to the facts.** It is human nature to create 'noise', to offer subjective opinion that makes it difficult to discern facts from fiction. It's irrelevant whether this subjectivity is caused by individual charisma, the need to be heard above others, the embellishment of a story, or simply someone needing to be right all of the time. In order to accurately piece together the whole picture of what happened at the accident, the officer needed not only to listen carefully to everyone's version of the events, but also to discern the facts in a disciplined fashion without being sidetracked by the noise.

3. **Watch for personal bias.** To randomly consider someone's version as right or wrong, or credible or not credible, is dismissive and potentially dangerous. This type of binary thinking leads to the omission of crucial facts, which in turn leads to defective conclusions.

⊰·⊱

When making decisions about how we want our future to look, it is preferable to base our decisions on factual information rather than conjecture. I'm certainly not encouraging conspiracy theories, but we shouldn't necessarily believe everything that we read, hear or see on television. If the information we need is important, it is better to take the time and trouble to verify the information by cross-checking it with the most reliable sources at our disposal. We can often only get to the real truth of the matter by triangulating information from several sources. Only then can it become consistent enough to be believable.

Ascertaining the truth or accuracy about something in life invariably requires us to stand back and look at the bigger picture in which the truth is lying. Always seek advice from credible people, and don't let your decisions be hijacked by your own emotional bias. Above all, stick to the facts – nothing shouts louder than the facts.

2

EDUCATION, EDUCATION AND EDUCATION

Our most valuable asset

> *A decent education is your international passport to a better life.*

There is simply no substitute to a comprehensive education. There are three reasons for this:

1. An appropriate education affords us the opportunity to secure a decent job – maybe even our dream job. Eventually, the income from our work can buy us the freedom to choose the life we want. That privilege is worth striving for.
2. Education is the mind food that fuels our personal growth. Our own individual development can be both personally satisfying and an attractive quality to those around us.
3. Education is a portable asset. What we embed in our brains is automatically transported with us wherever we go in this world. It's ours to keep, forever and wherever.

> *If we love what we do, we don't work a day in our lives, and we are likely to be good at our jobs.*

Ideally, we want to be jumping out of bed every morning, and fired up about going to work. Otherwise, for at least eight hours every day, we're just killing time doing soul-destroying work.

Unfortunately, there are simply no shortcuts to achieving educational and career success in our lives. We need to:

- Be organised.
- Do our research.
- Pay attention to the detail.
- Be conscientious.
- Be fully committed to the plan we have set for ourselves.

To this end we need to be mindful of the 6-P formula:

> *Proper Preparation Prevents a Pitifully Poor Performance.*

Socrates' famous saying: "To know thyself is the beginning of all wisdom," is right on the money. Most school-leavers understand little of who they are and what they want to do with their lives. This is because they may never have given it much thought, or perhaps they have had little school or parental guidance on the matter. If we walk into life with our blinkers on, trying to discover what we should be doing with our lives will, in the words of Confucius, be "like trying to find a black cat in a dark room". Unless we are extremely lucky, it will involve much trial and error, which can be costly, time-consuming and disheartening.

I strongly recommend that *before* leaving school, we consider putting ourselves through a battery of aptitude and personality tests. The results will indicate our strengths, weaknesses and personal preferences. This is usually a very enlightening exercise that quickly aligns us with a qualification that best suits our level of intellect and temperament. This in turn gives us the confidence to succeed in the direction of our choice and gets us off to a great start in an appropriately aligned career.

Welcome to 4th industrial revolution (4IR)

Like the previous three industrial revolutions, the first of which started in the late 1700s, this revolution, which started in the 2000s, is introducing new technologies that have already started to, and are continuing to, transform the world of work as we know it. It's almost happening at the speed of light.

4IR combines the physical, digital and biological worlds to usher in exciting new technologies. Examples of these include artificial intelligence; robotics; genetic engineering; blockchain; quantum computing; virtual reality; 3-D printing; biotechnology; renewable energies; composite materials; and the Internet of Things.

This tsunami of technology is permanently altering our global workscape. Millennials are the first generation to confront this new wave of work head-on, and it can be daunting. By quickly adapting to this technology, millennials can bypass the process of having to adopt older technology that would eventually have to be dumped to make way for the new. Spare a thought for the older baby boomers and generation Xers still in the workplace. They will need to radically reinvent themselves to stay in the game.

If, as I believe, our education is one of the most important investment decisions that we will make in our lives, then positioning ourselves for a 4IR future is a no-brainer. This does not mean that traditional career opportunities and their existing technologies will not be around for much longer. I think they will, but with 4IR looming large, a cornerstone of one's education should be anchored in this future reality. In 20 years' time, we still want to be employable, or at least familiar with the technology of the day. Careers that engage with contemporary technologies will, no doubt, offer the most attractive salaries, too.

Knowledge decay

There is, however, a complication *en route* to 4IR. It's called "the half-life of knowledge", a phrase coined by Samuel Arbesman and used as the title of his book.[8] Facts combined with other facts give us something meaningful, called information; and information combined with experience gives us something valuable, called knowledge. So if the underlying facts change, our knowledge no longer holds true. This is a sobering thought.

Arbesman's *Half-life of facts* is actually a metaphor for the half-life of the unstable elements found here on Earth, like uranium and thorium. Just as the unstable elements decay at a predictable rate over time, so, too, does our knowledge. What's more, the decay of our knowledge can happen at an alarming rate, as shown in the hard-hitting graph that follows.

FIGURE 1: The decay of knowledge

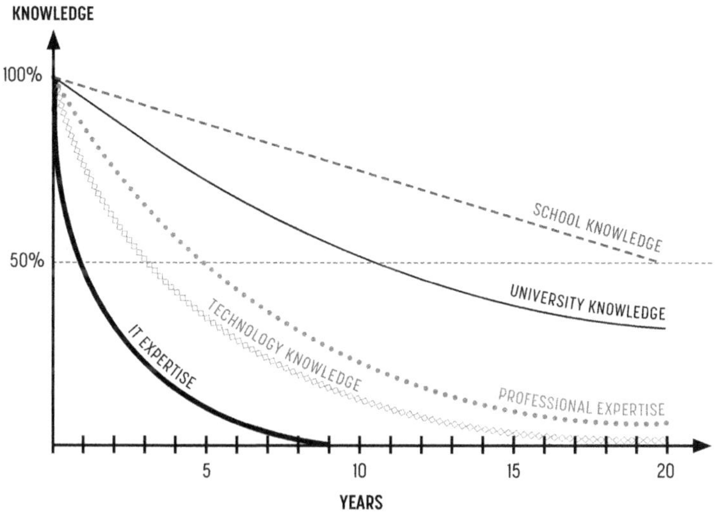

Source: www.ieee.org

---

8 Arbesman, S. *The Half-life of Knowledge*, Penguin Random House, 2012.

If we look at the University Knowledge line in the graph on the previous page, we will see that more than 60% of a person's university knowledge becomes redundant after just 20 years. If we think that's bad, look at the IT Expertise line in the graph – 100% redundant in only nine years! It does beg the question as to what experienced graduates can do about this.

It seems that our first tertiary qualification today is for *a time* – not for *all time*. To avoid irrelevancy, we will need to be courageous advocates of constantly re-educating and re-skilling ourselves. We will need to stay tuned in to relevant material in order to remain mentally agile and employable in the rapidly evolving world of work that awaits us. Fortune will favour the brave *and* the prepared.

⋄⋄

For decades, Kodak was a household name synonymous with anything to do with photographic film. Despite the onset of the digital era, Kodak executives did not believe that the era of digital photography would gain traction, notwithstanding all evidence to the contrary. On top of that, the Kodak company actually owned some of the digital photography technology, too. The executives folded their arms, buried their heads in the sand, and plodded on with the status quo. As Michael McQueen so aptly put it in his book *Winning the Battle for Relevance*[9], the Kodak company remained on autopilot until it flew into the side of the mountain. The corporate graveyard is littered with companies whose leaders failed to grasp the bigger picture and the importance of staying relevant.

⋄⋄

---

9   McQueen, M. *Winning the Battle for Relevance: Why even the greatest become obsolete... and how to avoid their fate*, BookBaby, 2013.

The moral of the story is that whether we are an individual or a company, we need to keep our eyes peeled on the horizon for the coming changes. The constant arrival of new technologies is making much of our previous knowledge redundant. As a result, we need to re-learn and reposition ourselves for a future that is a constantly moving target. It may be exhausting, but we don't have a choice if we want to stay current and reap the benefits of doing so.

The four cornerstones of education

There are four cornerstones in the development of our education and career. Two of these cornerstones have already been covered above. They are:

Cornerstone 1
Positioning ourselves with futuristic technology to remain relevant in the workplace of the future.

Cornerstone 2
Ensuring the currency of our knowledge by keeping up to date with the facts underpinning our knowledge.

A third cornerstone reveals itself in the story that follows:

<∰>∘<∰>

Einstein was once asked in a competition how many feet there were in a mile. He said that he didn't know. The quizmaster was agog that the maestro had been caught out on a relatively easy question. He asked him why he didn't know the answer. Einstein's retort was simply that he could find the answer to that question quite quickly in any standard reference book. He would far rather use his mind for creative purposes than as a "warehouse of facts".

Most facts today carry expiry tags, and there are simply too many of them bombarding us via social media platforms, 24-7, 365. What's more, we have the challenge of trying to establish fact from fiction as the world drowns in the propagation of fake news. The writing is on the wall: we can no longer absorb information in the way that we did before, so we can't really learn in quite the same manner that we did before. The quantum, type and pace at which the tidal wave of information is washing across the social media platforms and through our minds is unprecedented.

The old days of rote learning and regurgitating facts no longer suffice. Foundational facts are now available in a flash, thanks to the likes of Google. As demonstrated by Einstein, decluttering our minds and being more discerning about the knowledge we choose to synthesise is worth contemplating. By being creative, innovative and imaginative in our minds, we can produce higher-order thinking for the higher-order challenges that will most certainly be confronting us in the years to come. It was Albert Einstein himself who once famously said: "*Our problems will no longer be solvable at the same level of consciousness at which they were created.*" So, this gives rise to the third cornerstone.

Cornerstone 3
Adopting an appropriate methodology of thinking and learning, which we can then use as a powerful tool in our educational armoury going forward.

For example, an app like Blinkist allows us to read, in 15 minutes and at a fraction of the cost, a succinctly written summary of the major points of a book that would take an average of 10 hours just to read (not considering the time it would then take to extract all of the salient points from the book). This is an example of how, considering the time pressures we are facing, we can acquire and assimilate information in a far more efficient and effective way.

Cornerstone 4

Gaining expertise is purely a function of time.

This is assuming, of course, that we have applied our minds appropriately along the way, and that we have given our specific field of endeavour the focused attention it deserves.

Gone are the days when we could be a 'jack of all trades' and land a well-paying job. Today, this domain is largely reserved for the privileged few who have a multidisciplinary understanding of managing all aspects of major corporations around the world. We now live in an age of specialisation in which people dedicate themselves to focusing sharply on specific subject matter for much of their working lives.

The key to unlocking this specialised knowledge is not only the education that we have given ourselves, but also the time that we have afforded ourselves to acquire the necessary experience. According to Malcolm Gladwell in his book *Outliers: The Story of Success*[10], becoming a guru in a particular field requires applying our mind for at least 10 000 hours in our specific wheelhouse. That's a long time, but the point Gladwell makes is that there are no short cuts.

---

10 Gladwell, M. *Outliers: The Story of Success*, Little, Brown and Company, 2008.

So there you have them: the four cornerstones on which we can build a relevant and sustainable career via a flexible and largely specialised education.

Learning about learning

I will finish with a few of my own philosophical nuggets on matters of education.

1. **When we involve ourselves in the 'doing', our learning gains serious traction.** Consider the Confucian adage: "I hear, and I forget; I see, and I remember; I do, and I understand." It would be useful to remember this when teaching others.

2. **Let's guard against becoming professional students.** Some people spend their lives collecting degrees for academic purposes only. A vice-chancellor at a graduation ceremony I attended at Oxford University astutely remarked: "It is not what we know in this life, but what we *do* with what we know that really matters." In other words, it would be preferable to apply our knowledge rather than to just accrue it.

3. **The more we travel, the more worldly we become.** What we learn while travelling, especially internationally, cannot be taught in a classroom. Travel knowledge is worth its weight in gold. If anything is going to show you a bigger picture in this life, international travel is it. Well-travelled people are usually interesting people too.

4. **Let's not overlook the opportunity to consult with respected elders.** With the exception of those in more evolved societies, most elders today are shamefully relegated

to the sidelines of society. This brains trust can be found locked up in the older generations, vastly unappreciated for all it can offer. If we can access it, we would be wise to tap into this pool of knowledge. To have the wisdom of age and the energy of youth is to have the best of both worlds.

5. **The covert curriculum in most academic pursuits concerns human relations.** Life is still very much a question of who we know rather than what we know. Although Dale Carnegie's books, like *How to Win Friends and Influence People*[11], are somewhat dated now, their messages are still relevant today.

6. **The more we learn, the less we realize we know.** It should be incredibly humbling for all of us to realize that our understanding of this life is merely the tiniest tip of the iceberg. When we meet people who are gurus in their field, and it dawns on us that they have already forgotten what we still have to learn, that is the opportune moment to re-set our thinking on just how much there is to know out there.

7. **Gearing up for new types of intelligence.** Self-help books have, in recent decades, advocated that the three most important types of intelligence that we should try and accrue in our lives are intellectual intelligence (IQ); emotional intelligence (EQ); and spiritual intelligence (SQ). This book tries to do some justice to EQ (in chapter 4) and SQ (in chapter 7) in particular.

---

11 Carnegie, D. *How to Win Friends and Influence People*, Simon & Schuster, 1936.

However, there are several other types of intelligence worth pondering that have popped up in recent times. They are *adaptive intelligence*, which refers to our ability to adjust quickly to changing circumstances; *visionary intelligence*, which is our ability to see the bigger picture in life that provides context for the decisions we make; and *political intelligence*, which is our ability to navigate our way through a range of people's opinions, and then to be savvy enough to find middle ground between these opinions to take everyone forward together.

8. **Time is our most precious commodity, and it waits for nobody**. There's one thing we can be assured of: our lives will be gone in a flash, so let's use our time productively and wisely. Every day of our lives we are surrounded by a living laboratory; so let's look, listen and learn as much as we can, every minute of every day. Subscribing to the philosophy of lifelong learning is a valuable trait that we can nurture within ourselves. It underpins our personal growth, makes us interesting to others, and comes with substantial rewards over time.

3
MONEY MATTERS

Let's start this chapter by debunking a couple of myths.

Myth 1

The answer to life's problems is to make a quick buck.
There's no such thing as quick money! No one, but no one, gets wealthy quickly, unless they happen to be a trust-fund kid, a lottery winner or a criminal. Watch out for those unscrupulous people promising to make you a fortune overnight – it's just a crock of codswallop, and most likely a freshly concocted Ponzi scheme designed specifically to permanently rid you of your hard-earned, after-tax cash. The saying goes that if the offer is too good to be true, it usually is (not true). If you have any doubt about this whatsoever, google Bernie Madoff.

Incidentally, let's not waste our time and energy envying trust-fund children or lottery winners, either. These rare breeds haven't really earned their money, so they often find difficulty in valuing it. People who struggle to value their money usually can't hold on to it and their money quickly falls prey to that Chinese proverb: "Easy come, easy go."

Anything worth having in this life takes time to accumulate – especially when it comes to money and reputation.

Myth 2

My salary or monthly earnings will see me through to the end of my days.
Unless we're super-earners with large annual bonuses, this is a mistruth. Most salary-earners never retire with remotely the same standard of living they enjoyed up until the point of their

retirement. For many, the change in living standards is actually a cold shower just as they are supposedly heading into their golden years.

The deception of salary earnings is that our monthly pension deductions will be sufficient for our retirement, thanks to those 'experts' out there investing in 'reliable markets' on our behalf. The sobering news is that this is often not the case.

So, what's the bottom line here? Our salary should actually be our *cash cow* that funds the creation of our real wealth, which is made elsewhere.

Now please don't stress about the implications of possibly not having appreciated these two myths earlier in life. It's never too late to get our bucks in a row. Look at Colonel Sanders who started franchising Kentucky Fried Chicken (KFC) at the age of 62. Only when he sold it all out at 75 years of age did he become a financial icon.

Sometimes our upbringing doesn't sufficiently expose us to the art of making, keeping, managing and growing our money in this life. There's no need to beat ourselves up about it because it's not our fault. It just goes some way to explaining why fewer than 3% of people retire financially comfortable today.

Like anything worth having in this life, there is the *big picture*, and then there is the *detail* within that big picture, that we need to grasp to get our financial house in order.

Working the system

From a financial perspective, the big picture is that we have incarnated into what is essentially a material world: a capitalistic, economic system. We need to learn to deal with it, because we are ultimately responsible for our own financial wellbeing in this system. It is not an ideal system – not by a long chalk – but compared to socialism, capitalism has proven to be the lesser of the two evils. It is the system that offers a more favourable outcome to mankind, but only if we learn to work the system.

Importantly, capitalism requires us all to essentially play by the same set of rules. However, we need to be keenly aware that it favours those with education, money, ideas and the ability to borrow money to leverage opportunities.

Unfortunately, capitalism has had the unintended consequence of splitting the world into two camps: the 'haves' and the 'have-nots'. It's complicated, and a topic that can be better understood by reading the plethora of economic textbooks available on the topic. All I encourage us to do here is to get ourselves into the 'haves' camp.

If we start with the end in mind (the big picture), we really don't want to end up being in the 'have-nots' camp. Imagine discovering in our mid-60s, after working really hard all of our lives, that we do not have enough money to live on in our retirement. That's like sitting down to write a final exam that we have worked so hard for, only to find that we've learned the wrong stuff and can't recognise any of the questions. It's an eye-watering mismatch between expectation and a reality that we would rather avoid.

As part of coming to grips with the bigger picture of capitalism, I highly recommend reading the life stories of the fabulously wealthy dollar billionaires like Warren Buffett; Steve Jobs; Bill Gates; Elon Musk; Jack Ma and Aliko Dangote, to name just a few. It has taken them their lifetimes to accrue their wealth; and the best of their teachings can offer us so much about amplifying the right attitudes and skillsets to bring meaningful wealth into our lives, too.

Playing by the rules

Before I go into some of the detail about ideas for our long-term financial security, let me propose a few important ground rules.

1. **Ensure that we earn an honest buck.** Those who take short cuts live to regret them. I have seen this happen, time and again. The cosmic accountant's job is to keep our personal books permanently balanced. If we put something into our books that was never ours in the first place, the correction will come. It's just a matter of time.

2. **Pay our taxes timeously and in full!** Too many people start out not taking the taxman seriously enough and then burn their fingers. There is a distinct difference between 'tax avoidance' and 'tax evasion'. The former is legitimately minimising the tax that we have to pay; the latter is illegally paying less tax than is actually due by us. I have heard of people who evaded their tax for years, retired, and then got cleaned out by the tax authorities in their retirement. This is because unpaid taxes can be subjected to backdated penalties and interest that can strip us of every last cent we have. In the eyes of the courts, ignorance of the law is no excuse. If submitting correct tax returns is not our forte, it would be best to appoint a consultant to do the job for us. But remember this, too: the taxman will hold us, not our consultant, responsible for any unpaid taxes. When it comes to paying our due taxes, the buck stops with us – no one else.

3. **Know the difference between an appreciating asset and a depreciating asset.** Appreciating assets are those things that we buy that normally grow in value over time, like property and blue-chip stocks. Depreciating assets are those

things that we love to buy that lose their value quite quickly, like smart cars, fancy household appliances, and the latest cellphones and computers. Wise people ensure that most of their hard-earned, after-tax cash goes into appreciating assets, so that their money can grow with time. On the other hand, Joe Average uses his credit card (the bank's money) to buy things immediately that will lose value over time. What's more, he'll have little to show for it afterwards.

4. **Gather as much intelligence as possible on a potential investment.** The difference between a good and a bad investment often comes down to the amount of research we have done on a particular asset class, or its sub-classes. Before taking the plunge, an astute approach would be to do the research. The deeper we dig, the more intricacies we will uncover, and the more we can refine our approach to that investment. There is no short cut to doing extensive research and really understanding the investment we are contemplating.

5. **Understand that timing is everything.** I am a great believer in the cycles of life; those waves of events that come and go in repetitive patterns. The older we get, the easier it is for us to recognise them, especially when we catch ourselves saying: "I've seen this happen before, on more than one occasion." If we can first determine where in their cycles the economy, interest rates, and various asset classes are before making an investment, we can then optimise the timing of the investment we make. If we want to optimise the performance of our investment, we want to get in somewhere near the bottom of a cycle, and then out somewhere near the top of that cycle.

6. **Be aware of relevant inflation rates.** This will help us to understand the value of the financial returns on any of our investments. Put very simply, inflation is the degree to which the buying power of our money weakens as the cost of things around us rise. Any investment that returns a lower percentage to us than the inflation rate means that we have gone backwards financially. We must try to prevent the buying power of our money from being eroded in this manner.

10% of all we earn is ours to keep

It is time now to get into some practical detail of money matters.

To get off first base, we need some earning power. It is assumed here that we have now educated ourselves to find an appropriate vocation that provides us with a monthly income. By earning power, I mean the ability to earn reasonably consistently (month by month) *and* to have some money left over at the end of each month after we have paid all of our expenses.

I can hear you asking: "What do you mean money left over at the end of each month?"

The secret ingredient to financial success is, as stated: *10% of all we earn is ours to keep*. We should insist on making this happen for ourselves. To ensure that we do save at least 10% of our earnings at the end of each month, I suggest that we discipline ourselves by forcing this saving using a debit order on our account. We can then ensure that at least 10% of our earnings is automatically deducted from our accounts at the end of each month and moved to another account without us ever seeing it. When it's out of sight, it's out of mind.

There are a number of powerful reasons for doing this:

Reason 1

Discussing money and where to invest it is usually meaningless to those who have nothing to their name. It is only once we have saved a respectable amount of money by our own standards that our interest in money matters is awakened – and awaken we must if we want to become financially independent of others in our later years.

Reason 2

At some stage, life will unexpectedly confront us with unanticipated costs. If we don't have the money to meet those unforeseen financial obligations, things can get terribly stressful. If we have to borrow the money from someone else, it can carry with it emotional indebtedness and additional costs in the form of interest payments on the money borrowed. In the event of an unexpected cost, saved money buys us peace of mind, as we are able to settle those costs immediately. It is better to go backwards in savings than to put ourselves in debt.

Reason 3

One has to get around the adapted version of Parkinson's Law: "Our expenses increase to absorb the money available for them." In other words, the more we earn, the more we tend to spend. It is extremely easy to fritter away our extra earnings without even realising it. By taking off at least 10% of our earnings upfront, we can adapt to spending less. We simply learn to make ends meet with less every month.

Reason 4

By putting away at least 10% elsewhere, we set in motion a fabulous financial force. It works like this: only two things make you money in this life: *You* and *your money*. But we are already working hard to earn our keep every month, so we have taken care of that one. Now we need to get the other horse on to the racetrack: getting our money out there working hard for us every hour of every day, of every month, of every year. Money never sleeps. When we put that saved 10% into action elsewhere, like in a separate savings account to start with, we earn interest on that saved money.

At the end of the first month, the interest that we have earned is added to the initial 10% we put in. All of the interest earned thereafter is not only on the 10% saving lots that we are putting in every month, but also on all the previous months' interest lots that we are reinvesting into our savings account. That means we're earning interest on interest, commonly known as the magic of *compound interest*. By doing this, we have started a 'money tree' that will grow and multiply our money at an accelerating rate over the passage of time.

Reason 5

There will come a time when we need a lump sum of money to make an investment superior to the amount of interest we are earning from the money accruing in our savings account. Cash is king, especially in bad times. So, putting down a deposit for an investment property, for example, that we can buy relatively cheaply in bad times, might well lead to tenants paying a better rental return than what interest we could have earned in our savings account. This does not include any capital growth that we should accrue on the property when we decide to sell it.

By reinvesting our compounded savings into a more attractive asset class, we will have 'leveraged' our compounded 10% savings to get ourselves into an investment with a better return.

Once again, this is our money making us more money, while we are busy earning our 'salary' full-time elsewhere.

In summary then, at least 10% of what we earn is the *cash cow* that eventually helps us to financial freedom. As long as we remain disciplined in our monthly savings, and we invest our savings wisely over time, we should be able to retire comfortably without too many worries. We will also learn a lot along the way, and hopefully have plenty of fun, too. Consider the possibility of also being able to add a family inheritance or an incentive bonus from work to our cash pile. That sort of financial injection can help tremendously towards our next investment.

Investor or speculator?

So, where is it advisable to invest our first, and subsequent, piles of cash that we have been putting away religiously each month?

Well, our first and most important port of call would be to consider placing our savings into one of the major asset classes. We probably want to be invested in all of them eventually, but we need to start somewhere. Our starting point will most likely depend on our personal preferences and the cyclical opportunities that fortuitously present themselves when we have enough money to start investing.

The four major asset classes in which we can invest are:
- Property
- Government bonds
- Equities
- Cash.

With time, it would be preferable to invest in all of these asset classes in specific proportions, depending on our age, stage and personal risk profile. I am not going to go into any detail here on these asset classes or their sub-classes. That is not the purpose of this book, nor my area of expertise. Besides, there is already an abundance of information online that can educate you far better than I could on the breadth and depth of each asset class.

Some people feel the need to throw caution to the wind and take disproportionate risks by investing disproportionate amounts of their savings into financial instruments other than the major asset classes. Let's address this matter briefly.

Speculators can't resist the potential, juicy upside of a financial fling. After all, it's their own money, and they can do what they like with it. Note that I said their 'own money'. As long as they do not break the golden rule of speculating with borrowed money that belongs to the bank, then they must do what they need to do. However, if you happen to be the speculative type, may I suggest that you carefully consider the following.

If you take a considerable financial risk in a gambling house (which I consider to be an absolute den of iniquity), you may be 'lucky' enough to win something in the short term. But in the long term, you will give it all back to the house, with interest. Gambling machines are designed to take our money from us. The croupier nearly always ends with the upper hand at the card tables, too. I think it would be better to keep gambling to a once-a-year outing only. That's it! And if you have an addictive personality, it's best to avoid gambling altogether.

If you cannot resist taking a 'calculated risk', then rather consider taking only 5% of your total financial portfolio's value to do so. Call that your High-risk Trading Portfolio, rather than your High-risk Investment Portfolio. Trading is not investing. Always be very mindful of the fact that you are speculating with your hard-earned, after-tax cash. The financial instruments for high-risk money are usually some derivative, like options and futures on bonds and equities that can offer very substantial rewards – and very substantial losses. Very short-term, intra-day speculative opportunities can also be attractive, with the likes of currencies, crypto currencies and highly traded shares on the stock market. If the markets are particularly volatile, then it can be speculation on steroids.

In my younger 'cowboy' days, when I believed I was infallible and could beat the markets blindfolded, I learned some crushingly painful lessons. It only takes a single large trading position to go south for one to quickly learn the uncomfortable outer limits of one's risk appetite.

In a nutshell, the problem with speculating is that when we take that intended quick position on a financial instrument, there are usually just too many unknown variables and unanticipated events at play which can temporarily – or permanently – trash our position.

⋘·⋙

I once bought shares in a gold mine for short-term speculative purposes, but a fire broke out on the mine the day after my acquisition. The mine closed down and the share was 'suspended' for several weeks. When the mine started up again, the share price opened sharply lower, and I was forced to sell a few weeks later after losing 30% of my money.

Another share I bought suffered a similar fate and dropped 20% in one day after a prominent politician was assassinated in our country.

The infamous Nick Leeson brought the whole of Barings Bank to its knees when the 7.2 Kobe earthquake unexpectedly rattled the Japanese markets and obliterated Leeson's short-term position.

When COVID-19 struck, all world markets fell off a precipice, and anyone who had taken a quick flutter in the market just before that, must have experienced massive financial losses in their portfolios.

⋞⋟∘⋞⋟

Who could have anticipated any of those events? Just be aware that there is a plethora of unknown economic and financial information emerging on a daily basis that can directly impact our financial position. It's worth considering that anything worth having in this life takes time to accumulate. It can't be done in a rush. When we invest in something, we are actually in it for the long haul.

Property prospects

I would like to take you through the story of an investment in residential properties I made over a 12-year period. Since it turned out reasonably well, I would like to put it under the microscope in order to emphasise the salient points that I have been attempting to address in this chapter.

⋞⋟∘⋞⋟

By my mid-40s, I had saved some salary money, received a helpful inheritance, and sold my quarter-share in a factory building that I had helped to construct 10 years earlier. At the time, I had read a very well-researched government report that had predicted a massive semigration to the part of the country in which I live. I reasoned that this was bound to put upward pressure on housing in our neck of the woods, particularly as our city had recently become one of the social capitals of the world.

However, the global financial crisis of late 2008 had just struck, and the liquidity in the global financial system had dried up. People in our country became nervous and started selling off investment properties for fear of losing their jobs and not being able to meet their monthly mortgage repayments, which depressed local property prices. Interest rates started to come down as the government tried to kickstart the flagging economy.

At the time, I lived literally five minutes from the university – an institution that had the best global ranking of any university in the country. There was always a shortage of student accommodation for the university, and the situation seemed to get worse every year. My wife, who worked at the university, kept me informed about how the university's management was planning to massively increase its enrolment numbers.

Having attended that university myself, and having lived in the suburb in which it was located for most of my life, I knew the geography of the area extremely well. When it comes to property, it's all about location, location and location.

My wife and I were both experienced in renovating homes and enjoyed the creativity of the process. We were quite content with buying a two-bedroom apartment with a view to immediately adding value to the property by turning it into a three-bedroom apartment. I had saved enough money for us to carry out the construction process. I calculated that by collecting an extra rental every month from the additional bedroom, we could alleviate the monthly mortgage payments to the bank to such an extent that we would probably break even within two years of buying the property.

However, our plan would require me to buy the property at a discount, and importantly, to research the regulations of the body corporate of the apartment complex to see if the conversion was legitimate, according to its specific rules. I would also have to get the timing of the purchase right by waiting for the three-month legal transfer period to happen, and then get the renovation done in time to find suitable students before the start of the academic year. There was a lot at play, and we needed to get the timing of each activity spot-on.

I presented my idea to my local bank manager and her team. They were very thorough in their assessment of whether I could qualify to borrow money from them. They checked my financial track record to ensure that I was not blacklisted with any of the credit bureaus; and that none of my payments had 'bounced' in the past five years. They checked that I had sufficient cashflow to fund the property purchase and renovations, and to pay the full monthly mortgage amount for six months, in the event I could not find tenants to take immediate occupation of the apartment. They called for my spreadsheet, which itemised my three-year income and expenses that demonstrated the apartment's potential financial viability by the end of that period. They were happy on all counts, and granted me a bond on the property. So, I bought my first apartment.

As I invested more and more in the property asset class over the years, I started to appreciate the inner workings of our financial system. The following financial insights were of major value:

Insight 1
Without borrowing money from banks, it's almost impossible to buy large appreciating assets, like properties. But you need some cash upfront, or the appropriate security, to be able to leverage money from the bank in the first place. This shows again how important it is to get that first lump sum saving up and running, predominantly, from your monthly income.

Insight 2
Banks like to lend money to organised people, and preferably to those who have multiple sources of income. Every time I bought a property, I added another rental income stream, which made banks even more comfortable with loaning me additional money.

Insight 3
As the underlying value of properties usually grows over time, banks recognise the accruing capital gain on them. Bankers then factor this capital gain in as further collateral for themselves, which in turn enables them to lend even more

money to qualifying clients for their subsequent property purchases. It's a lending system that starts to fuel itself.

Insight 4
Putting all of the properties into one profit and loss account allowed me to cross-subsidise the costs of newly-purchased properties with the surplus income of previously-acquired properties, thereby optimising my cashflow and minimising my tax payments. It also made any unexpected cost, such as a special levy on one of the properties, relatively easy to absorb.

Insight 5
In theory, the more properties that I bought, the more the banks supported my future property purchases. I soon realised that the financial system in which I was living favoured those who had the capital to get started. I call this the snowball effect, after the Warren Buffet biography, *The Snowball*[12], in which he demonstrated quite clearly how money makes more money. It dawned on me that, unless we take charge of our own financial destiny early on in our lives, we can't hope to experience the kind of financial accruals that the system has to offer.

Insight 6
When I started selling my property portfolio because the market had turned, I finally understood why business schools around the world teach that if we want to make real money, we need to go out and sell our businesses. When we sell investment assets, we pay a capital gains tax on the financial gains made. This capital gains tax rate is normally a much lower tax rate than the income tax rate that we would have paid had we earned the same amount of money as part of our salary. We can read and understand this in economics textbooks, but experiencing it in practice really rams the point home.

---

12 Schroeder, A. *The Snowball: Warren Buffet and The Business of Life*, Bantam Books, 2008.

Eight years and nine apartments later, it was unfortunately time to rethink my property investment strategy. Although property prices had risen prominently, along with the apartments' rental prices since purchasing them, the cool winds of change had started blowing steadily through my investment plan. As the saying goes, nothing lasts forever, and we have to be agile when it's time to change speed and direction.

The university was experiencing all sorts of unexpected student demonstrations over #feesmustfall, and the security and safety of the tenants and my properties became a concern. The quality of the tenants I was attracting was declining, and some started defaulting on their rentals. Interest rates started picking up, too. Costs like municipal rates and apartment levies, which were beyond my control, were escalating faster than the inflation rate. Government policies threatening property rights were also becoming a serious concern for all property investors around the country, regardless of whether they were in residential, commercial or industrial property portfolios. And the country's currency was fast losing ground in the international marketplace. Sadly, the big picture in which my investment had been comfortably nestled seemed to be turning sour, and fast. It was time to cash up and get out.

At the time of writing this book (during COVID-19), I still had a few properties left to offload. In such a scenario, you soon appreciate how relatively illiquid real estate is. One can't quickly convert a large asset like property into cash, especially in a time of doom and gloom. I should have started offloading the apartments a year or two earlier, when things were peaking, but hindsight is a perfect science.

I am not prepared to hang in and ride this down cycle, because I am 59 years old, and I don't believe the country, over the next 10-15 years, will dig itself out of the mess it has got itself into. By then, I hope to be slotting quietly into retirement without any worries about aberrant tenants, failing government policies and a mauled local currency.

Personal financial housekeeping

The art of financial housekeeping is managing our money via strong domestic budgeting. It's the fastest way to detect 'money leaks' in the system. Increasing our earnings and reducing our expenses is the basic formula to effectively running any successful budget.

We should also be looking out for that 'dead money' that lies around in our homes. These can be household assets, such as paintings, antiques, and tarpaulin-covered cars which lie tucked away gathering dust somewhere on the property. If we do not use or value such items every day, it would be best to sell them and add the cash to our savings.

There are also other ways to improve our home budget situation. These include taking advantage of domestically-orientated tax breaks, like working from home. It is worth finding out what is offered by the tax authorities in the country in which you live.

> *Prudent financial management is about putting away money on a monthly basis for that treat we need to give to ourselves.*

It's important psychology to reward ourselves for taking a constantly disciplined approach to managing our money. I found that saving for an annual family holiday did the trick for me. When it's time to pay the travel agent for that magical getaway, having the cash at the ready makes the world of difference.

Just a caveat: try not to become caught up in the 'scarcity mentality'. This is a state of mind in which we cannot bring ourselves to spend money on anything considered non-essential. We can save ourselves rich, but that's a painful route marked by deprivation and a poor quality of life. Besides, most people don't want to be around those who constantly claim that they cannot afford to pay for their fair share of things. So fanatical can this approach become that, when such people many years later eventually find themselves in a position that they *can* actually afford non-essential items, like holidays and treats for themselves, they just cannot bring themselves to part with their money. Look out for the balance of spending money versus saving money. In that way, you will bank many happy memories.

Keep records

It's really valuable to keep financial records – and relatively easy to do so these days on a computer spreadsheet. Updating our net asset value (what we own minus what we owe) can come in handy, especially when we need to borrow money from a bank. Record-keeping is normally obligatory for the taxman. We need to account for the taxes we have paid in the past (for up to five years, at least, in most cases) should the taxman query anything.

We might want to take advantage of any tax breaks on offer for making improvements to our homes. If so, we need to have kept all of our building contractors' invoices and our proof of payments to them. If our house should happen to burn down and we want to be justly remunerated for any destroyed items, fire insurance policies require us to have itemised and authentically valued everything in our home. Without going overboard about it, determine what will be worth recording so that you can at least protect your hard-earned, financial position.

Gone are the days when we could shove our blue-chip share certificates into the bottom drawer and forget about them. These days, the investment world changes too fast to enjoy that bygone luxury. We need to keep our hands on the wheel of our financial activities, and mindfully manage the risks that crop up along the way. Besides, we don't want to miss superior opportunities when they present themselves.

By the way, it's worth thinking very carefully about whether we should ever become a minor shareholder in a private company. In such a position, we don't enjoy influential decision rights, and our money can be locked up for years without anyone being interested in buying us out of our position. If you decide to run your own business one day, remember these words that I once saw on an accountant's desk: "Turnover is vanity, profit is sanity and cashflow is reality."

On a final note, Mahatma Gandhi said: *"There is enough for every man's need, but not for every man's greed"*. Avarice has been the downfall of many souls who have lost their way and their fortune because they could not determine what enough was.

If we start early in our lives with a financial plan, and we work steadily towards our financial goals over the years, there should be no need for any greed at any stage.

4

EMOTIONAL COMPETENCE: OUR NUMBER ONE LIFESKILL

A people's world

> *Our golden key to happiness is our ability to forge meaningful relationships with others.*

No matter where we go and what we do in this life, the art of interacting successfully with others is fundamental to our wellbeing. The people who come into our lives – whether for a reason, season or a lifetime – can bring variety, interest, learning, friendship, love and joy.

So, how do we become uber-competent in our relationships with others? Well, let's stand back and look at the bigger picture: there are apparently about seven different life competencies for which we should strive: linguistic; logic; kinaesthetic; spatial; musical; intrapersonal; and interpersonal competencies.

In my view, two of these competencies trump all of the others put together. Combined, they give us the edge in our relationships with others, something called 'emotional competence'. Daniel Goleman was a pioneer in this field and called it emotional intelligence, or EQ.[13] These two competencies are:

1. **Intrapersonal awareness.** This skill helps us come to terms with who we are, what makes us tick, how we can become our own best friend, and how to progress to being a well-adjusted individual in society. I consider this to be so important that I have made it an underlying theme throughout this book. It forms the bedrock on which we can build incredible contentment in our own lives.

---

13 Goleman, G. *Emotional Intelligence*, Bloomsbury,1996.

2. **Interpersonal proficiency.** This is the skill of getting on well with those around us. Once we have our own house in order, we should find it easier to interact more comfortably with our partners, children, family, friends, work colleagues and strangers. When we learn to connect emotionally with others in such a way that they feel at ease with us, trust us, and look forward to engaging with us, then that, too, can enrich our lives beyond measure.

I am certainly not suggesting that we have to kowtow to anyone to get them to like us. On the contrary, I'm talking about engaging with others confidently, and on an equal footing, regardless of their station in life.

Unfortunately, there has been a tendency over time to overemphasise the value of having a strong intelligence quotient (IQ) at the expense of having a robust emotional quotient (EQ). This is a great pity, because I have seen too many intellectually smart people render their contributions meaningless as a result of their offensive behaviour in front of others.

It most certainly does help to be cerebrally smart in this world, but if we believe that we can get away with relying solely on our intellectual prowess, we are mistaken. Our intellectual horsepower may be one thing, but our connection to others and the social contentment that it brings, is quite another. While the two should certainly not be confused, attaining both might be considered having the best of both worlds.

Let's also be mindful of the fact that it is far easier to plant our ideas in the minds of those who are already receptive to us. For this reason, it makes sense to sell ourselves first, and then our smart ideas second.

Recurring blindspots

The analogy of a blindspot is an interesting one. If we do not have a specially configured side mirror on our car that exposes the natural blindspot while driving, we endanger ourselves and others on the road. The same principle applies to us and our emotions. If we do not have a well-developed, internal ability to calibrate the emotions that drive what we say and do, we endanger our relationship with others, as well as ourselves.

⊰≽·≼⊱

> I was talking to a senior executive one day when his cellphone rang. Mid-conversation, he took out his phone, looked at the screen, answered the call, and sauntered off to have a discussion with the caller. He left me stranded, mid-sentence, with not the slightest hint of an apology for interrupting our discussion; nor any indication whether he would return.
>
> In that moment, his rudeness made me feel unimportant and dispensable. I understood immediately why that executive was so unpopular in the organisation. He clearly had no social graces, and he had, over time, left far too many people reeling in his wake. It wasn't long before he left the company. I heard years later how he had wandered from company to company without gaining much traction anywhere.
>
> Some days later, I recall standing in an airport bus, waiting to be taxied to our plane. Over the heads of my fellow passengers, I caught the eye of a friend of mine, who was a senior executive in the financial world. He had just put his phone to his ear to make a call, but the moment he made eye contact with me, he killed the call, grabbed his bag, and made his way towards me through the throng of passengers. We shook hands and had a lovely conversation in which we shared much of what had been happening in our lives.

It's not surprising that my friend went on to become hugely successful in the financial world. People of that ilk command the salaries that they want to earn.

However, the former executive was oblivious to how his behaviour was chasing others away from him – despite his apparent intellect and the fact that he held a senior position in the company. Such people are blind to their brand of antisocial behaviour, which systematically sabotages their relationships with others.

⋙·⋘

But let's not pretend to be perfect – many of us allow our emotions to go rogue on us. There are two common features about people's emotional blindspots that are useful to know.

Firstly, there are at least half a dozen emotional blindspots that commonly trip up many of us. Secondly, these blindspots often have invisible packaging, and they lie in waiting to ambush us when we least expect it. It's awkward, because we don't see ourselves clearly enough to recognise that these sorts of behaviours can really put people off wanting to be with us.

The good news is that we can rid ourselves of them, but we first need to know that they exist. Once we are aware of them, we can then clear their debris off our runways so that we can go places in life.

Let's look at five of the more common blindspots to which people fall prey.

Two ears and one mouth

Blindspot 1 entraps those of us who battle to listen properly to others.
You would think that being able to actively listen to someone is a relatively simple thing to do, but it's not. It doesn't seem to come naturally to many people.

Instead, many of us end up interrupting those who are speaking without letting them finish what they are saying. When we interrupt others, we disturb their train of thought, and important bits of information get 'lost'. This is frustrating to those who are trying to be heard.

The act of 'hearing' someone talk is one thing; but the art of 'listening' earnestly to what someone is saying is quite another. Listening intently to others can be really hard work, especially when we're trying to listen at 'different levels' to what is actually behind the words being said. Our ears are not ornaments; they are indispensable antennae capable of tuning into every nuance of every word that is uttered in our direction.

For any relationship to be meaningful and sustainable, its dialogue should resemble that of a two-way street.

> *We have two ears and one mouth, and it would be preferable to use them in that ratio.*

If we apply that principle, we will be doing more listening than talking, and that's a good thing.

Most of us have experienced what it's like being in the company of a 'motor-mouth' – that person who simply won't stop talking. It can be frustrating and exhausting, especially when they don't even pause between sentences to draw breath!

Such behaviour is actually quite selfish, because it prevents others from participating in the conversation. People like that can end up losing their audience, sometimes permanently.

As a motivation to encourage ourselves to be better listeners in the future, there are two compelling reasons to listen more attentively to others. Firstly, we learn precious little by doing all of the talking; but there is no limit to what we can learn by doing more of the listening. Secondly, we immeasurably endear ourselves to others when we listen intently to what they have to say. Ironically, this is probably because they are not used to being given the floor by others. When we allow others the opportunity to speak to us in an uninterrupted fashion, they really appreciate it.

Biting our tongues

Blindspot 2 ensnares those who seem intent on constantly criticising others.
We do not win friends and influence people by finding fault with them. In fact, by being a constant critic of others, we are signalling something quite unpleasant about ourselves to all those around us.

If we should ever catch ourselves criticising others, especially behind their backs, let's rather bite our tongues. If we were to anyway look more closely at what our critical words would have been, we would be surprised to find how frequently our criticism amounts to hypocrisy.

> *If we look closely enough, we are often guilty of the very things we accuse others of being and doing.*

There is no upside to finding fault with others; so let's refrain from it entirely.

If we are going to criticise someone because it's absolutely necessary, or circumstances dictate that we should, then may I suggest two courses of action: have the discussion face-to-face with the person involved, and then package it diplomatically and constructively for them. Done that way, we might actually be thanked for our feedback.

When we are on the receiving end of some throat-choking critique, the best approach is not to consider criticism as a personal attack. Otherwise, we could become super-defensive, even hostile. In that critical moment, rather take a deep breath and consider that taking foul-tasting medicine is not very pleasant, but it usually makes us better.

It's a strange phenomenon, but many people have a propensity to criticise others rather than to compliment them. Why not find reasons to compliment people rather than to criticise them? Have you ever noticed what often happens when we shine the complimentary spotlight on others? If you observe closely enough, you will notice that people tend to dismiss compliments by downplaying them, ignoring them, or completely changing the subject away from them. Tragically, this is most likely because they are simply not accustomed to receiving compliments, and they have no experience in how to respond appropriately to them.

The heartwarming part of paying someone a compliment is witnessing how it can bring out the best in them. For those of us who have received accolades, we know the feeling: it's wonderful! It boosts our self-confidence, and makes us feel really good about ourselves. We become quick to appreciate the person who has taken the trouble to recognise our efforts.

> *The interesting thing about paying compliments is that it costs absolutely nothing – just a tiny bit of our time.*

If we really understood the difference that compliments made in the lives of others, we would ensure that we dished out at least one compliment every day. As long as compliments are given sincerely, there is absolutely no reason to hold back on them.

The bane of know-it-alls

Blindspot 3 trips up those who seem to know everything.
Maybe we are one of those who have had a super-privileged education. Maybe we do know a lot, possess a well-above-average knowledge, and have a need to share it with everyone. Maybe we are also extremely articulate, have the 'teacher' within us, and feel like we're doing everyone a favour by ensuring they're better informed – because we know it all!

Let's be real: we're under a massive illusion if we think that there is ever sufficient justification to pontificate to others. Our audience won't see it that way. Chances are, they will see someone who arrogantly dumps their uninvited superiority complex right in the middle of other people's conversations. Know-it-alls are conversation killers, and they are easily recognisable by their trademark response of: "I know," which completes just about everyone else's sentences.

Isn't it amazing how two different schools of thought can see the same situation so differently? Even if we do possess a well-above-average knowledge, we should avoid falling into the trap of becoming a know-it-all. It is ultimately an illusion for the following reasons.

> *The more we learn, the less we realise we actually know.*

It's something of an irony then that those who seem to know it all have apparently stopped learning.

Fostering a culture of lifelong learning is critical to the evolution of our thinking. Being an eternal student of this life requires a degree of mental and emotional stamina that will continually test us. This is especially the case in a fast-changing world where information is quickly becoming redundant. Let's rather protect our minds from becoming stale, lacking creative thought, clinging to old ideas, and pulling rank with seniority. These are all symptoms of a stagnant mind.

Perhaps the better outlook to have is to ask ourselves when we last read a self-help book, registered for a short course, advanced our formal qualifications, learned a new language, or changed jobs.

If you have come across know-it-alls in your life – which I am sure you have – just remember how they made you feel, and learn from their mistakes.

Sorry really is the hardest word

Blindspot 4 trumps those who are unable to say sorry, even when in the wrong.

> *He who fails to apologise fails to take responsibility for the mistake that he has made.*

If you think about it clinically, it's actually quite fraudulent to claim that we are not responsible or accountable for an error that we have made. If we conduct ourselves like this in front of emotionally astute people, we will be revealing an awful lot about ourselves.

So, why do people opt out of apologising when the truth is ready to set them free?

It's probably the tyranny of the ego. It can be humiliating for someone to have to own up to a mistake. Perhaps they don't want to be thought of as a bad person for making a mistake, or maybe they don't want to expose the fact that they're not perfect. It could be that they're afraid of getting into trouble for being wrong about something important. There could be a myriad reasons.

The important thing to recognise is that part of being human is making mistakes. It's a powerful way to learn, but only if we are willing to take the lessons.

People who apologise unreservedly and unconditionally get the respect they deserve. If an apology is conveyed timeously and with sincere regret, people are usually more than happy to forgive and forget – sometimes even with a little bit of admiration for the person who has been prepared to gobble mouthfuls of humble pie in front of their detractors.

Finally, we shouldn't expect our apology to be completely accepted until we have proven ourselves willing and able to correct our aberrant behaviour. People are quick to see when we are just paying lip service to an apology.

Trumped by technology

Blindspot 5 corners those who allow technology to trump their relationships.

In a world where advancing technology dictates an ever-increasing pace of life, there is a compulsive need for people to seek instant gratification. Social media platforms gluttonously steal people's time and attention, and people want immediate responses to things – they're no longer prepared to wait.

Our cellphone and email etiquette are daily reminders of how we value the pace of life, rather than the quality of life, and the casualties are our personal relationships. They are being 'virtualised' and, dare I say, stunted by these instant technologies. In many cases, the younger generations are becoming addicted to technology, as they participate mindlessly in the busyness of life.

These technologies are certainly useful tools, but we need to give them their rightful place – not a dominant space – in our lives.

When practising delayed gratification, it is patience that will give us the perspective we need. All of those things worth having in this life take time to accumulate. I am not referring here to the amassing of material wealth, but rather to the accrual of lifeskills, people skills, friendships and value systems.

There is no quick fix to acquiring the important stuff in this life.

> *We cannot acquire people skills by downloading them on to our screens.*

Perhaps you think that I am rather old-fashioned for saying this, but technology really is hijacking our relationships today – and it's not a good thing.

For those who are striving for a better balance in their lives, toning down compulsive technology needs, climbing off the instant gratification bus, and sucking more on the marrow of life is where it can be found.

A tactical response to emotional hijacking

We've established that our relationships with others are fundamental to our wellbeing, and we've also determined that many of us fall into similar emotional traps that compromise our interactions with others. Five common blindspots have been tabled to demonstrate this point.

It was Robert Browning who said: *"When a man's fight starts with himself, he is worth something."* I therefore propose that we tackle our emotional fault lines head-on by adopting the following four tactics.

Tactic 1

To be able to decipher where our emotional strengths and weaknesses lie, and what tends to cripple our conversations with others, we need insight into our own emotional make-up. This can be extremely difficult because we don't 'see' ourselves clearly.

We therefore need to become fiercely introspective of our emotional anatomies by taking stock of our faulty thinking; the destructive emotions that arise from this thinking; and the offensive behaviours that follow and serve to undermine our relationships with others.

Thanks to the advent of smart phones, seeing our *physical* selves is easy enough; but seeing our *emotional* selves is quite another story. It's possible, but requires some delicate manoeuvering.

Let's take a quick look at a few techniques that will help us to see our emotional selves a little more clearly. Be warned, though: taking a peek inside our minds means fiddling with a few 'sensitive' neurons – something akin to tinkering with a car engine that's still running.

- **Ask a trusted friend or colleague how they experience you emotionally.** It must be someone without any vested interests in giving you the candid feedback you're seeking. As tempting as it may be to ignore the feedback because it is not what you want to hear, it's preferable to accept it for the invaluable gift that it is. Your children in particular are in a unique position to offer you unfiltered feedback without them even being invited to do so – and it's usually right on the money. Regardless of how uncomfortable the feedback is, it would be unwise to shoot the messenger. Rather just listen, take note, digest what has been said, and then let it marinade in your mind for a few days before reacting to it.

- **Practise meditation.** This healing technique will be explored in a little more depth later in the book, but meditation is magic in the making. When done regularly and effectively, it can bring extraordinary clarity to your mind. Immersing yourself into a high-quality meditative state helps you to be much more objective about yourself. It can really shift your thinking. A sufficiently relaxed mind can open wide enough to admit new thoughts and ideas that favourably alter your perspective on things – including yourself.

- **Take tests to measure your emotional competence.** If your intention is to get professional guidance to help clear the emotional debris that's polluting your mind, it will definitely be worth submitting yourself to such testing.

Tactic 2

Having compiled a list of the emotional shortcomings that tend to damage our relationships with others, we then need to motivate ourselves to act on that list! To enjoy the benefits of great relationships with others, we need to prevent ourselves from being hijacked by the emotional scarecrows that chase people away from us.

Crucially, we must *want to*, and be *able to*, successfully help ourselves. Otherwise, our efforts will quickly run out of steam and end up being in vain.

Finding a powerful enough reason to get cracking on our own emotional healing is all about establishing what will motivate us to jump off that couch and into action. Lasting motivation comes from within; so we all need to find and flick that internal mind switch that will bring about the required changes. That switch is in different places for different people.

- For born go-getters, the switch is permanently on, and they just get it done.
- Procrastinators need someone to push them hard to take the necessary steps to get it done.
- Those who are fearful will need to recall earlier statements

in this book: "Action cures fear," so they should "just do it!" There will be time to think about the consequences later.
- For those suffering from excusitis, they should jolt themselves into the reality that if they don't get it done, loneliness might just become their best friend.
- Finally, for those who feel they can't financially afford the help, they should tell themselves that they simply can't afford *not* to get this done – and then make a financial plan!

Tactic 3

Once we are sufficiently pumped up to want to make the changes to our emotional constitutions, we need to *make the changes*. Sometimes, one or two small self-adjustments in our own behaviour is all that is needed to make the world of difference to our interactions with others.

Alternatively, we can try rewiring our own thinking by implementing the offerings of neurolinguistic programming, or NLP. It's a widely accepted technique to help reconstruct our thinking and stop unhelpful behaviours from eclipsing our relationships.

Our habits can be so hardwired into us by our past that they are like stubbornly ingrained splinters in our minds. It is comforting to know that we are all products of our past, and that sometimes we carry a small measure of dysfunctionality as a result. Although this is quite normal, it can be a nuisance. Cumbersome emotions can get in the way of easy fixes.

As a result, we may need to resort to 'processing' our emotions rather than 'intellectualising' them, which is not for the fainthearted. The fix usually comes in the form of therapy, like psychotherapy or hypnotherapy, and it needs careful orchestration by a professional. Therapy can be quite emotionally taxing, so expect to shed a few tears during the sessions, but it is the best solution, and offers a lifetime of reward. I can personally attest to the fact that it's well worth the investment.

After dissolving our destructive emotional behaviours, we will have positioned ourselves to ascend on an entirely different emotional trajectory. We will then be free to attract a new spectrum of people into our orbit.

We were designed to be social creatures. It is our natural way of being. The English poet, John Donne, famously recognised this when he wrote: *"No Man is an Island."*

Tactic 4

We are now at liberty to go out there and shop around for a powerful assortment of people skills that will attract others into our lives on a more permanent and meaningful basis.

While the purpose here is certainly not to trawl through what constitutes 'the ultimate compilation of social skills for connecting successfully to others', here are a few emotional competencies to ponder when connecting with others in new ways:

- Remaining upbeat and cheerful for much of the time.
- Staying calm under pressure.
- Being assertive rather than aggressive.
- Being flexible and co-operative in situations.
- Being consistently respectful towards others.
- Being responsible for our own behaviour.
- Having a warm and appropriate sense of humour.
- Doing good deeds for others.

- Being an astute interpreter of other people's body language.
- Asking for help when we need it.
- Ignoring unwanted peer pressure.
- Finding reasons to compliment people rather than to criticise them.
- Listening well without interrupting others.
- Giving credit to others rather than taking it for ourselves.
- Understanding the difference between sympathy and empathy.

The last point is an important one. The following incident might help explain the difference between sympathy and empathy:

<><>

When my wife broke her shoulder during a fall, she was in agony for the first few days. Her prescription drugs kept some of her pain at bay, but she had difficulty sleeping. She was unable to find a comfortable enough position in which she could fall asleep. During that early period, she received a number of WhatsApp messages from friends, two of which demonstrated the difference between sympathy and empathy.

The first message read: *Hi Gail. Sorry to hear you hurt your shoulder, hey. Can you send me the address of that plumber you said did a good job for you guys, please? Our geyser has packed up.*

The second message read: *Shoo Gaily! I heard you broke your shoulder while running yesterday. That must be really sore. I know you won't be able to cook dinner tonight, so I'm gonna make something for you guys and pop around with it in a couple of hours. Do you need something from the pharmacy because you'll need to keep that pain under control for a few days. Hang in there, it will get better. Thinking of you.* ♥

<><>

The contrast between the two messages highlights the difference between 'sympathy' in the first message, and 'empathy' in the second. These two words have entirely different meanings and entirely different impacts.

Sympathy is a matter of giving a brief thought to someone else's situation – in this case, recognising that Gail had 'hurt her shoulder'.

Empathy, on the other hand, is when you can almost feel someone else's pain – in this case, recognising that Gail's shoulder 'must be really sore'. Those who are empathetic have the capacity to walk in the emotional moccasins of others. They identify strongly with how someone's pain is affecting their life. Those who truly empathise will often physically follow through with demonstrable support that underscores their empathy – in this case, offering to bring dinner. This is empathy in action.

Emotional competence is undoubtedly the next frontier in this world.

> *Nurturing sincere and unselfish concern for the welfare of others is one of the most powerful emotional competencies we can develop. It's a social skill that creates friends for life.*

In recent times, we have seen how famous politicians, sportsmen, businessmen, movie producers, actors, clergymen and government officials have systematically fallen from grace. Whether they have compromised their self-proclaimed values or let slip, for example, their racist, sexist, fascist or homophobic thoughts, it has boiled down to one common denominator: offensive emotional behaviour.

Embarrassingly, many of these people have had their emotional transgressions aired on international TV networks and on global social media platforms. Some of them end up apologising in the hope of being reinstated in the minds of the public, but they don't realise the damage they've already done. It is forever a stain on the minds of those who once held them in high regard.

Let's rather work hard to be exemplars of strong emotional competence. It will pay handsome dividends. It will also endear us to others on a more lasting basis, and allow us to befriend those who can bring great joy into our lives.

It is, after all, a people's world in which we live.

5

ATTRACTING THE LOVE WE DESERVE

The naivety of youth

For those of us who can look back at the heady days of our early 20s, it seemed like nothing could stop us. As we marched confidently into the future with qualification in one hand and the keys to life in the other, the road ahead seemed paved with plans and possibilities aplenty.

Yet most of us back then were oblivious to our reality. We knew precious little about life, even less about ourselves, and almost nothing about relationships – least of all one that could potentially last for 50 years or longer.

In our roaring 20s back then, life served up a seductive cocktail – and still does in my view – called 'YouthQuake'. Its ingredients are unmistakable: wall-to-wall parties lubricated with rivers of booze; scantily clad partygoers perfumed to the nines; bodies gyrating to throbbing music on strobe-lit floors; biological clocks ticking with rampant hormones; and raw biology succumbing to the inevitable, trumping all logic and sensibility.

In the blink of an eye, the ring arrives, the bells toll, and the keys to suburban living are secured with kidlets clinging to their parents' ankles.

That is all too often how it happened, and still happens – quickly, and without much thought, since this part of life is rarely found in any school syllabus. As the marital years unfold, couples are largely left to discover whether or not Lady Luck will smile favourably upon them.

For those looking back, take some comfort from John Lennon's words: '*Life is what happens while we're busy making other plans*'. It was hardly anyone's fault.

For those still fortunate enough to be navigating their twenties, you have the opportunity to shove aside societal pressures; disregard the bane of the biological clock; educate yourself on the covert curriculum of life; and circumvent the traditional, social entrapment described above.

Trappings of young love

There are three major hurdles that need to be jumped before we can better manage this thing called 'love'. If we wish to kiss fewer frogs on the path to true love, then the sooner we overcome these hurdles, the better.

The **first hurdle** is ensuring that, from day one, we go into our romantic liaisons with our eyes wide open.

What we witnesssed in our formative years, among our family and friends, and from films we watched, was probably an extremely limited – if not distorted – version of Love 101. However, those teachings were most likely all that was on offer to us at the time.

When our hormones eventually kicked in – along with their bed partners of peer pressure, biological clocks and unwanted parental guidance – life thrust us onto centre stage of what I like to call 'Love Unplugged'. It was like being on autopilot as we landed up in someone else's arms, trumped by our emotions and our physical responses to them.

'Love Unplugged' is the state of being completely overwhelmed emotionally, but utterly disconnected mentally from the reality of our situation. If and when the dalliance crumbled, we were left to pick up the pieces. Break-ups such as these were the breeding grounds for our self-doubting fears to loom large.

Not surprisingly, many of us didn't rush out for the next date, choosing instead to lick our wounds in the comfort of our own homes.

But let's not beat ourselves up about this. At that age, we were learning on the job, so to speak. Here is an analogy that tries to emphasise the importance of 'knowing what we're getting into' when our hearts start to flutter.

It is said that an electorate gets the government it deserves. Voters who are uninformed tend to cast their ballots blindly. This situation is exacerbated when they vote with a herd mentality, having easily been persuaded by others on how to vote. The result is that an inappropriate government takes root, which can be bad news for an electorate that comes to its senses too late. Governments elected in this manner can end up being abusive towards their citizens.

In a similar vein, lovers get the relationships they deserve. In other words, people who go blindly into romantic relationships with no understanding of what they're getting themselves into, can be in for a rude awakening. Instances in which a lover has allowed society, family or friends to pressure them into a relationship with someone else, can land up being in abusive relationships – and unhappy marriages.

When we engage romantically with someone, it is preferable to switch from autopilot to manual. We need to appreciate that our inexperience makes us vulnerable. To consider our safety and wellbeing at all times, we must judge the situation with our heart and our head. We need to know that we can still have fun while acting rationally. The younger we are, the more we need to be aware of just how much we still don't know about love. It is wise, therefore, to proceed into the lovers' den with a healthy dose of excitement combined with some self-respect and caution.

The **second hurdle** to clear is realising the business we're in when we're romantically involved with someone – and that business may actually come as something of a surprise to many. Paul Hauck in his masterpiece *How to Love and Be Loved*, eloquently but bluntly states the order of business when it comes to matters of love:

"When we sweep all the hearts and flowers of a relationship to one side, we actually have quite a hard-nosed business arrangement – it's about satisfying each other's most important needs."[14]

Hauck advocates that we're actually in the "loving business", not in some fluffy, dream state, floating atop cloud nine. We can certainly have our heads in the clouds every now and then, just as long as our feet remain firmly on the ground.

This may sound quite callous, but there's no need to feel uncomfortable or deceived by this – it's simply the nature of all functional and healthy partnerships. If both parties end up reciprocally getting what they want out of a relationship, then it's a win-win scenario that cannot be achieved by either party on their own.

It helps to share candidly with your loved one what it is that you most value from your relationship with them. Otherwise, the quality of your relationship is likely to be a hit-and-miss affair. Once you have clearly established each other's needs, then the next challenge is to ensure that you are both *capable* of satisfying those needs. Finally, you must be *willing* to satisfy each other's needs. If the relationship is to be sustainable, it would be preferable to do this on an unconditional and continuous basis.

---

[14] Hauck, P. *How to Love and Be Loved (Overcoming Common Problems)*, Sheldon Press, 1983.

> *Compatibility has always been, and will always be, the crucial ingredient of a successful relationship. It's as essential as clean air is to healthy living.*

If there is not enough compatibility, recognise that fact and then act on it straight away by quietly excusing yourself from the relationship. That will be better in the long run for both parties.

By the way, we shouldn't be alarmed at how different people's needs are from one another. For example, if a woman says she wants to be materially comfortable in a relationship, and that she expects the man to provide for her in this regard, then he needs to decide whether or not he's up for it. Otherwise he can be fairly sure that if the money dries up, her love for him will fly out the window faster than he can say: "Knife!"

I heard of an amusing situation some years ago. A middle-aged divorcée was on the prowl for a man of means in our neighbourhood. She was an attractive and wealthy cougar in her own right. One day, she finally met her beau, and he was soon seen ferrying her around in a fancy Porsche and wining and dining her at all of the right places. It was a whirlwind romance, and in a matter of weeks, they had tied the knot.

The day after they signed the nuptial contract, he unabashedly handed his Porsche back to the car hire company and surrendered his maxed-out credit cards to the banks. Needless to say, shortly thereafter, they found themselves in the divorce courts. The message here is that we might want to be a little more circumspect about what we wish for in our relationships.

The **final hurdle** that we need to clear is overcoming the fear of being jilted by our lover. The thought of not being loved or wanted by our partner any longer is, quite frankly, a dagger in the heart for most of us – especially where there's no apparent reason and no explanation given. People can go to extraordinary lengths to avoid being dumped by their lover – to the point of even abandoning their value systems and behaving out of character. Rejection is the ace in the relationship pack that trumps most of us. If we have a fragile ego, a lot of suppressed fears can rush to the surface if and when this happens.

Let's have a look at this poem that I wrote, called 'The Miracle Cure', to hopefully get some more insight on this delicate matter.

Like a long forgotten story it begins to unfold
Of two little earthlings whose love is foretold;
Is it written in the stars or part of destiny
That their paths should cross so interestingly?

Whisked through the gates of Golden Cupidville
Where euphoria abounds and time stands still;
Soulfully engaged in their intimate dance
Would that such bliss were an eternal trance.

But in the cycles of life with its ebbs and its flows
Is the sting of the thorn and the smell of the rose;
The dualistic nature of all things impermanent
But for steadfast love anchored in the firmament.

In risking love we reveal all our fears
Emotional baggage carried through the years;
Rejection presents that fork in the road
A gift from heaven to lighten our load.

Brave is the soul that embraces the mirror
Reflecting these struggles that it must consider;
To see or not to see, the ego will decide
Will it evolve or will it hide?

When the pupil is ready, the teacher will appear
Master in disguise to those in despair;
The lessons are painful so be sure to endure
And experience the wonder of the miracle cure.

This Teacher of true love, the cosmic glue
More so in adversity will stick by you;
To love and be loved, this is your goal
To sing and dance to the music of your soul.

To understand love, we need to experience it. However, we can only experience it if we are prepared to risk loving someone. In taking that leap of faith to love someone, we make ourselves vulnerable to being rejected by that person.

If we love and care for ourselves deeply enough, being jilted by someone else shouldn't be too big a deal in our lives. Sure, if we are smitten with that person, we'll be miserable for a while, but it's not the end of the world, and it certainly won't be if we care for and love ourselves deeply enough. That's the secret ingredient: being sufficiently happy within yourself so as not to be derailed by someone who's no longer happy with you.

If, after being spurned by a lover, we are going to get back on to the horse and ride confidently into our next relationship, we will need a strong sense of self-respect. This is not to suggest that we should be narcissistic. Rather, we should care deeply enough about ourselves not to be held to ransom by what someone else happens to think or say about us. While cruel words uttered in our direction can be very destructive, we cannot be harmed by these words *unless* we give them the emotional power to do so. That's the choice we have to make, and only we can make it.

If someone treats us badly to begin with, we can simply turn the other cheek. If they continue to treat us badly despite our protestations, we need to forgive them, for they realise not what they do. That is the time to get up and move on from the abuse, because they are the one with the problem. It's critical that we are able to do this, because if we don't get up and move on, then people could fairly suggest that perhaps *we* are the ones who have the problem.

> *We need to think more highly of ourselves and not let others talk down at us or walk all over us. We can only genuinely love others in the future to the extent that we have been able to truly forgive ourselves and others in the past.*

When we are young, we have the uncanny knack of attracting those people into our lives who reflect back at us the very issues we need to resolve within ourselves. As we soldier on from one relationship to the next, we can be forgiven for thinking that all relationships are just one big merry-go-round – and a lot of hard work! But if we learn quickly from each relationship, our courage will, in time, connect us with someone who has similar values, interests and preferences. We will just know and feel, at a cellular level, when we have met someone who is our equal. That someone will respect us, empower us and have our back at all times. In short, it will be someone who turns out to be our lover and best friend; someone who complements our own happiness and has the potential to be our lifelong partner. This is when we will start to experience what 'authentic love' really has to offer.

So, let's take the sting out of love, and start choosing our partners wisely. After educating ourselves (Chapter 2), choosing a lifelong partner is probably the second most important decision that we'll make in our lifetime.

Choosing a lifelong partner

Most eligible bachelors and bachelorettes spend an inordinate amount of time and emotional energy trying to find love – sometimes quite frantically through a process of trial and error.

> *When it comes to matters of the heart, it is better to take our time and make an informed decision than it is to make a very costly error of judgment too early on in life.*

Before rushing headlong into a romantic liaison, take time to consider on which principles you could base your future relationships.

Here are 12 principles for you to ponder before jumping into any serious dating scene:

1. **Get your own house in order first.**
   Go off and experience relationships; travel as much as you can; and earn some money before settling down. It's an opportunity to knock off some of those rough edges that stick to us early in life. The learning curve of our 20s will anyway accelerate at an exponential rate; and we can hardly

expect two people's interests to match and accelerate in the same direction and at the same pace for their entire 20s – there is simply too much on offer and too much going on during that decade of exploration. It's better to wait until we're 30-something before contemplating settling down with someone else. Like a good red wine, we will need some maturation time before anyone can enjoy our taste.

2. **Become your own best friend.**
The most misunderstood concept about a relationship is that our partner is responsible for making us happy in life. This could not be further from the truth. Our contentment needs to be self-generated. We need to walk into a relationship as own best friend already. From there on, our partner just adds to, or complements, our own happiness. There's a good reason for this: if we are depending on our partner to make us happy, but for some reason our happiness is no longer on their agenda, then we're in for a miserable time.

3. **Become friends before lovers.**
Falling in lust is easy, but falling out of lust can be tricky. Sexual chemistry can be really sticky stuff from which to extricate oneself. When we realise that there are actually no long-term prospects for the relationship, we should not allow ourselves to get caught up in the relationship for the wrong reasons. Let's save ourselves from all the heartache caused by diving too quickly into a relationship. It's much simpler to just be friends at first, and then to let the friendship gradually evolve into something more substantial – as long as the feeling is mutual.

4. **Like attracts like.**

   It may sound boring to an outsider when you tell them that you and your partner laugh and cry at the same things; enjoy similar activities together; watch the same genre of movies; listen to the same type of music; read comparable books; have similar educational backgrounds; and enjoy a shared group of friends. But actually, that's far from boring. When we have so much in common with our partner, life together is compatible, uncomplicated and fun. That's how we want it to be. I don't buy into the notion that 'opposites attract'. Any dating duo locked into that drama has many issues on both sides that need sorting out. Cross-cultural relationships can work, but for reasons similar to opposites attracting, they can be harder work than they need be.

5. **People who share the same values share a comfortable relationship.**

   There's a lightness of being between two people who are in sync. They're not worrying about watching their backs all the time, or wondering whether one of them is going to let the other down again. Values such as honesty; reliability; stability; empathy; emotional availability; loyalty; commitment and fidelity are the bedrock of any solid relationship. A sense of humour can be a real tonic too. When things get tense between couples, which happens, a well-timed and appropriate sense of humour can be very disarming. So, let's be on the lookout for these relationship values and nurture them as best we can.

6. **A relationship is only as good as its dialogue.**

   Being able to converse regularly with our partner about all aspects of the relationship is key to its success. Conversation is to a relationship what air is to life. Without it, our relationships suffocate. Importantly, dialogue is a two-way street, so best we give our partner a lot of space to verbalise their thoughts and feelings. While plenty of dialogue is a quintessential ingredient to any successful relationship, remember, too, that there can be harmony in silence.

7. **Great couples empower one another.**
Most relationships have, to some degree, an imbalance of power within them. If the relationship is to survive and thrive, it is up to the more dominant person to recognise this and ensure that the power is evenly distributed. It is a real treat to watch a mature couple stepping aside for one another, giving each other the floor, and not interrupting one another when doing so. Conversely, there is nothing more debilitating than witnessing two people continuously carping at one another, and constantly criticising and blaming one another over petty issues. It invariably becomes embarrassing for others around them.

8. **We need to accept our partners the way they are.**
It is preferable not to try to change our partners to suit ourselves, or to think that we can change someone for the better by becoming their in-house therapist. We must be sufficiently happy with what we see upfront, because that's what we're going to get, warts and all. As John Legend's lyrics so poignantly advise us, we need to love our partner's "perfect imperfections". Of course this does not mean that we cannot express our dissatisfaction if our partner develops an irritating habit or an unacceptable behaviour. Holding up the mirror for our partner when something has become distasteful is actually an act of love, especially when it is done kindly.

9. **Agreeing to disagree respectfully.**
It is vital that couples have their own voices within a relationship. It is not only healthy to hold different opinions from one another on particular topics; it is also respectful to listen to each other's points of view especially when accompanied by robust debate. Being able to compromise and pursue conciliatory solutions is a powerful antidote to the trials and tribulations of forging a strong partnership.

10. **Interdependence is the happy equilibrium.**
As we have said, to be entirely dependent on someone else for our own happiness is unhealthy. In the same vein, to be totally independent from our partner's opinion in major decision-making matters will also be detrimental to the relationship. Interdependence is when we combine our efforts to achieve a higher middle ground that would not be possible by attempts of either individual on their own. It's a win-win scenario that underscores the great advantage of playing as a couple.

11. **Appreciating the differences.**
Many books have researched the fact that healthy differences do exist between men and women. Men and women can approach money, sex, clothes, tidiness and arguments wildly differently from one another. It doesn't make the one right and the other wrong, it simply makes them different in how they see things and do things. The key for lovers, regardless of their sexual orientation, is to appreciate their differences, work with them, allow them to be expressed, and to adopt the best perspectives from both contributions. Couples would do well to do everything in their power to prevent healthy differences from unnecessarily ambushing their relationships.

12. **Addictive personalities are high maintenance.**
Be cautious of getting involved with someone who has an addiction to the likes of narcotics, alcohol, gambling, gaming or social media. If our partner has an addictive personality, we can expect to constantly play second fiddle to that addiction, regardless of the potential we may see in them. An adaptation of a Shakespearian adage says that 'hell maketh no music like a partner playing second fiddle.' Unless we are alive to these dynamics, our value system will most likely be repeatedly compromised, and we will be let down more often than not. It may be wiser to walk away from it because it's a hard slog to nowhere that will invariably end in tears.

If, after at least a year of being in a committed relationship with someone, you are seriously considering taking things further, there are still a few recommendations that I would like to make.

- It might be prudent to check with a few of our more candid family or friends whether they think our personality has changed since dating our partner. If, according to them, we have either stayed the same or changed for the better, that's a positive sign. If, however, we have changed for the worse, let's strongly re-evaluate our next steps.
- Comprehensive questionnaires on the compatibility of couples are available via marriage counsellors. These may be helpful tools to get another more objective view on our relationships.
- Travelling together away from home for a while means that we don't have access to our normal domestic comforts and fallback positions. This can be a litmus test in determining the strength of our bond and our resolve to help one another

when faced with unfamiliar or difficult circumstances. True character is often revealed under such circumstances, especially when the chips are down.

- Although orthodox religious thinking might frown on this suggestion, it is preferable for a couple to trial living together for a year under the same roof before making a decision to walk down the aisle together. Too often we hear of couples who dated for years, got married, and then six months after living together, parted ways. Shared living – especially in confined spaces – can project new dynamics on to our relationships that we could not reasonably have anticipated.
- We need to establish whether we are sexually compatible with our partners, because we cannot really afford for that part of our relationship to be problematic. Good chemistry is usually the accelerant that ignites a couple's passion for one another. However, there's a big difference between having sex twice a day as opposed to twice a month. And if we're not into the *Fifty Shades of Grey* thing, best we know this up front, too!
- Research suggests that there are six contentious areas of cohabitation or marriage. It would be prudent to know about them and to discuss them in our courting phase. They are religion; money; sex; careers; children (especially how many you want to have, and the disciplining of them); and socialising (especially with family).
- When it comes to family, the apple usually doesn't fall far from the tree. One can sometimes get a glimpse of how our partner may turn out in the future by looking at our partner's parents. However, we should also be mindful of how successfully people can break the mould of their upbringing.

For the love of marriage

Many young people today are questioning the very institution of marriage. They argue that it's now the era of 'friends with benefits' and suggest, among other things, that sex is freely available to them; that it's now acceptable for children to be born out of wedlock; that financial success is more quickly attainable to single-minded men and women who are instead married to their jobs; that regular and extensive travel should not be shelved; that independence and freedom should be valued; and that instances of divorce are now even more prolific than ever.

Although this is quite a compelling list of arguments, my short answer to them would be that they must go off and do what they've got to do. However, on their travels, they might like to contemplate the following:

Men and women are essentially gregarious creatures. They ultimately seek to socialise and are instinctively programmed to mate and have offspring. They also want to protect and nurture their young, but they need each other in close proximity to successfully do this. The unique human trait of aspiring to higher ideals is more readily achieved and enjoyed when it is accomplished with someone else, rather than alone. But the trump card here is love, and all that it can reveal in the intimate dance between two people.

Unfortunately, when we are young and inexperienced, the concept of love can be misunderstood and misrepresented. For example, the belief that love involves giving endlessly to our partner without expecting anything in return is quite common; but quite frankly, it's nonsensical. Only slaves do that. While giving to our partner is important, to suggest that it is done under slave-type conditions is a misrepresentation of what true love really is. Giving is certainly a loving act, but there comes a time when not giving can actually be the most appropriate love act of all.

Similarly, those who feel that love has abandoned their relationship as soon as the head-over-heels obsession fades, have misinterpreted the meaning of authentic love. The euphoric mist of infatuation – call it lust, if you will – eventually evaporates. But as it burns off, it can make way for other types of love to muscle in and flourish on a more sustainable basis – but only if the participants have the proclivity to explore further.

We need look no further than the ancient Greeks and Romans to get a richer understanding of the word "love" and all of its underlying meanings. These ancient civilisations mythologised the various kinds of love through the plethora of gods and goddesses they worshipped. The ancient Greeks specifically divided love into eight different types of human emotions. I liken these many types of love to the many facets of a diamond. When all of the facets have been polished, light pours through them into the centre of the diamond, bursting into an array of dazzling colours. It is this brilliant, multicoloured sparkle of the nuptial jewel that symbolises the bringing together of all the facets of love that the union of marriage can offer its occupants.

Let's take a brief moment here to table the Greeks' interpretation of love. The purpose is not only to appreciate the breadth and depth of its meaning; but also to appreciate the various emotions that the 'love' word evokes.

The first type of love is **ludus**, which means "school", or "game" in Greek. I like to think of this as the stage at which we are schooled in the game of love. It's a phase characterised by playfulness, flirting and lightness of heart – to the the point of experiencing that heart-wrenchingly naïve 'crush' on someone.

It is essentially the innocent affection displayed by two people who feel the dance of attraction between one another.

The second type of love is **Eros**, named after the Greek god of fertility, and from which the English word "erotic" originates. This is the passionate and magnetic attraction that occurs between two lovers who engage physically with one another. It is the sexual chemistry that forms the glue for something more substantial, should the lovers choose to take the relationship to the next level. Of course, it includes the possibility of procreation.

The third type of love is **philautia**, which is self-love. This might sound somewhat narcissistic, but as mentioned before, it's an extremely healthy form of self-respect, or self-care. It's about feeling comfortable in our own skin, liking ourselves a lot, and being our own best friend *before* engaging intimately with others. Greek Philosopher Aristotle, said: *"All friendly feelings for others are an extension of our own feeling for ourselves."* It's akin to sorting ourselves out first before being able to put our best foot forward for others. It's the vaccination against rejection. Getting successfully through this phase of self-love is the biggest hurdle for people to clear in attaining true love and happiness with someone else in their life.

The fourth type of love is **philia**, which is the deep friendship experienced between close friends. It transcends physical attraction and is associated more with the common interests that exist between two people that make their companionship exceptionally meaningful. It's that bond between two people that strengthens over time and makes them want to go the extra mile for one another.

The fifth type of love is **storge**, which is the deep affection that family members feel for each other. By extension, it is the devotion that we have towards our children that is instinctively protective, nurturing, forgiving and free of expectation. It is the care that goes beyond the call of duty to put us right at the side of those who need us. This emotion is felt in our allegiance towards a team (or a family) of which we are a member, or even a country towards which we are very patriotic.

The sixth type of love is **pragma**, from which we get the English word "pragmatic". This word means to engage in situations sensibly and practically, and implies that a person has sufficient experience to realistically know how best to manage a situation. Importantly, it is a position that is taken in the long-term interests of someone. It is a mature, emotional response that understands compromise, patience and tolerance in a relationship.

The seventh type of love is **agape**, the unselfish concern for the welfare of others. It is the feeling of oneness between family, friends, strangers, nature and God. It is the selfless and unconditional feeling of affection, empathy and compassion towards every sentient being. It is the highest order of love available to us, especially when connecting with our divinity.

There is an eighth type of love which the Greeks called **mania,** but this is an excessively fixated, unhealthy emotion. I only include it here because the Greeks recognised it as a form of 'love', albeit a wayward type of emotion that is dominated by jealousy, co-dependence, stalking behaviour and even violence. I suppose that these emotions are experienced when someone has become fanatically obsessed with another, but this is not love. It's a destructive emotional behaviour that is best avoided.

It is beyond the scope of this book to delve any deeper into these seven aspects of love, but suffice to say that the institution of marriage offers deep-dive opportunities to experience these love-based emotions.

When we look back at our first romantic experiences, they can often be likened to watching a grainy, silent, black-and-white movie in an overcrowded hall of people, where films were reeled through a film projector that broke down every now and then. Our romantic experience after a decade or two of blissful marriage is like watching a 3-D, colour movie, streamed with full Dolby surround sound into a comfortable, home movie theatre.

Conscious uncoupling

Falling in love is easy; and if you vaguely subscribe to the recommendations offered earlier in this chapter, hopefully you will be able to give this section of the book a wide berth.

However, falling out of love – and separating on a permanent basis – is not that easy, especially if a couple has been an 'item' for a long time. It's an emotional rollercoaster for most people who would rather be anaesthetised to the whole process than have to endure the harsh realities of 'uncoupling', as it was so famously euphemised in the 1940s.

But why is the divorce rate skyrocketing these days compared to previous generations? I think there are a myriad of reasons, but two overarching ones come to mind: firstly, the divorce rate is an indictment of the frenetic pace of modern living and all of the distractions that come with it. Secondly, it is the result of an out-of-touch education system that is not preparing us for life's big challenges.

Some cynics would even suggest that the institution of marriage was designed for people when their life expectancy was less than half what it is today. So, to expect couples to stay together for 50 years or more now is simply unreasonable and unrealistic. In my view, that's mischievous thinking.

Regardless of the reasons, falling out of love is simply not an easy issue to deal with in our lives. It is one of life's greatest heartaches, so it would be remiss of me not to include it in this book. Let's cover the subject as briefly and as constructively as possible. My aim is to equip the reader with some tools to help manage the process of separation more comfortably, should it come their way.

I think it is important to understand from the outset that the dissolution of a marriage or lengthy partnership whose contract has naturally expired, offers a massive opportunity to a parting couple to reinvent themselves; to fine-tune what makes them happy in this life; and to discover new aspects of themselves that they never knew existed (or had forgotten about). Both my wife and I are now in our second marriage, and after 20 years together, we remain very happily ensconced with one another. Take heart: I think many of us do things better the second time round.

The separation of a couple is the closing of a door to an old life, and the opening of another door to a new life. Sometimes the old door closes with great difficulty, gets stuck, or even falls off its hinges. Similarly, the new door can almost feel locked at times, or at the very least, stiff to open. Walking through these doors is a very tough transition, but it's a necessary passage to a new lease on life.

People find it naturally awkward to discuss the process of divorce when they are in the throes of getting married. But couples today are legally advised to be more pragmatic than their forefathers in their approach to prenuptial contracts. If and when couples reach that moment of separation, they will need the comfort of a prenuptial blueprint to guide them through what is traditionally terribly tricky territory to navigate. People's emotions often run too high for them to think logically or to behave rationally in such situations.

My first recommendation is to get a prenuptial contract in place that takes the sting out of any debate about who gets what; who goes where; who arbitrates the process; and who will pay. There is actually no reason to make a separation or divorce more of a headache than it is already renowned for being.

Whether two people come through a divorce feeling relieved or resentful is entirely dependent on the attitude they take during the process. There's always a choice for both parties. Either they can decide to carefully scale the slippery slope to higher ground and then move on as friends; or they can dive into the mud, get stuck, and live to regret the mudslinging. Without a shadow of doubt, I am an advocate for the former for the following reason:

> *The person we once chose to live with forever – now the person that we supposedly cannot live with ever again – was **our choice** in the first place!*

So, if we are going to criticise, insult, denigrate or publicly trash our ex-partner, we are simply announcing – via a megaphone to everyone – what a poor judge of character we were in the first place. Yes, people do change; and yes, we could argue that he or she changed so dramatically that they became insufferable. But I believe that very few incidents in life can change a person so utterly that he or she no longer represents the person that we married. It is more an indication that one, or both of us, still had our blinkers on when we Romeo'd and Juliette'd each other; or that we did not deal directly with the changing dynamics of our relationship when they manifested earlier.

If our relationship is that bad, and we don't believe it can be repaired, it is better to admit our mistake, take full responsibility for it, and get out – even if it is just for the sake of our own dignity and self-worth. Otherwise, we are responsible for aiding and abetting what can become a very toxic situation.

> *Think about it this way: marriage without the joy of love and friendship is a procrastination of the inevitable.*

Let's rather accept when we have outgrown the relationship – or the relationship has outgrown us – and give our marriage the decent burial it deserves. Life is too short to have regrets, be vengeful, or to constantly tolerate any form of mediocrity.

Polished in the tumbler

In most instances of divorce, there is little chance of avoiding the pain experienced in cutting up the marital asset cake. It is also made heart-wrenchingly more difficult when children are amongst the 'assets'. Sometimes I wish that I had been exposed to this kind of information before I went through the wringer myself. But, as they say in the classics, being put in the tumbler gives one the opportunity to emerge more polished, rather than being crushed into pieces.

What follows are some thoughts on aspects of separation that may be useful.

1. **Prioritising the children.**
   Bump the children to the top of the priority list and consider their needs first, above everything else. If necessary, have the children counselled to determine neutrally and professionally what their wishes are. Once there is resolution in this department, everything else will fall into place around the decisions of who will be their future custodian, and how the children will divide their time between the parents going forward.

   Children capable of verbalising their thoughts and feelings normally choose to go the parent to whom they are emotionally closest. No one has automatic right of custody of their children because of their position in the family, their gender or their financial status. If they're old enough, the kid(s) will decide; their best interests come first.

   I believe that those parents who stubbornly resist this approach attract nasty karma towards themselves. To use children as canon fodder during the breakdown of a marriage is to actually abuse the privilege of being blessed with them in the first place. It can also bring vengeful teenagers and young adults back into their lives with problems many times the size of their divorce-related difficulties.

   Look after the children's interests first, even if it requires more compromise than would ever have been considered possible before. It will save the family a truckload of self-inflicted heartache in the long run.

2. **Paying a high price.**
   Divorce will be as costly as we insist on making it. If we believe that the law only has sharp teeth when an expensive

lawyer is involved, then best we ready ourselves to literally throw away our hard-earned, after-tax cash.

Would it not be preferable to put all of those potential legal fees into a trust fund that could guarantee the children's future education; and have the separation mediated or arbitrated instead?

I suspect that there are many litigious lawyers out there who literally bank on a divorcing couple's emotional constitution remaining weak. For as long as an attorney can convince us that we can financially nail our ex-partner to the floorboards – after all, if our only tool is a hammer, every problem looks like a nail – then money will drain out of our bank account faster than we can sign the divorce papers. There is no victory in divorce. Squandering mountains of money as a result of being emotionally reckless is just a dreadful waste.

3. **Cutting up the marital asset cake.**
The fight for our so-called 'rightful share' of the marital assets (including alimony or maintenance) is, in most cases, just a grab at some insurance policy that life after divorce will be no less materially comfortable than life before the divorce.

It is human nature to want familiar comforts, and to want almost everything back the way it was before the divorce – but without the other person. Unfortunately, this is very rarely possible after a divorce.

As soon as aggrieved couples peer over the precipice of divorce, they must know that a substantial drop in their standard of living is imminent. The sooner they can come to terms with this and ready themselves for the pending financial dip in their lives, the sooner they can make their way to higher financial ground on the other side of divorce.

4. **Consulting professionals.**
   During the turmoil of divorce, it is very tempting to pour out our troubled hearts to an unsuspecting public, including our family and friends. At best, we will surreptitiously attract – and at worst actively recruit – those people who will tell us what we want to hear.

   There is no point in taking part in an exercise of self-deceit. Quite frankly, it's a little inconsiderate to dump all of our emotional baggage on others, especially if they never asked for it in the first place.

   Let's rather seek solace in professional people. It is their job to listen carefully to us, give us appropriate advice and respect the confidentiality of our thoughts. Besides, we need to hear a more objective opinion than that of our friends, too. There are three sides to every story: our side, our ex-partner's side, and the truth somewhere in between.

5. **Sticking to the truth.**
   In desperate times, people can resort to desperate measures. In a veiled attempt to manipulate the outcome of our divorce in our favour, we may be tempted to handle the truth awkwardly with those who are trying to help us resolve the dispute.

   This could include lying by omission, where we neglect (subliminally or in a calculated fashion) to declare relevant or accurate information to those trying to negotiate a fair outcome for us. This is disrespectful and unhelpful towards them. The truth, anyway, has an uncanny habit of eventually coming out into the open. Therefore, all that we will have achieved is to have alienated or to have left a sour taste in the mouths of those trying to help us.

   It is incumbent on us to conduct ourselves in a morally correct manner. We owe it to ourselves, our ex-partners and

our children (if we have any). In doing this, our integrity will remain intact, and we will have fewer regrets later. The truth is also easy to defend.

6. **Keeping our health in check.**
It is no secret that divorce can be an emotionally and mentally debilitating experience. While our spirit may be willing – and possibly even misguided while fighting tooth and nail for what we *think* is rightfully ours – our flesh is ultimately weak.

It is a lesser-known but universal truth that if we are emotionally traumatised for too long, we will find ourselves becoming physically ill. The two are inextricably linked. We need to preserve our health in these times by employing techniques to remain as stress-free as possible. This will include exercising daily and eating healthily.

If we do find ourselves in a very fragile state, I recommend that we *meditate* rather than *medicate* our way out of our predicaments. People who medicate are invariably held hostage by the drugs on which they rely. I recall a doctor once telling me that most medicines are actually poisons with useful side-effects. On the other hand, people who meditate are often pleasantly surprised at the freedom and relief that they discover in a quietened mind. Most importantly, exercise patience. It invariably gives the perspective needed in such times.

7. **Sticking to a divorce framework.**
No two separations are ever the same. Therefore, to extrapolate the outcomes of other divorce cases and to apply them to one's own case would be a futile exercise. It is likely to lead to unmet expectations.

There is, however, a general framework in which one can work, and it would be sensible to stick to this. It entails, among other smaller issues, what the law of the country in which the marriage took place dictates; the content of the marriage contract; the reasons surrounding the divorce; the emotional stability of each partner; and the age and gender of the children.

The rest is just noise.

8. **Mediating or arbitrating.**
Surprisingly, mediation and arbitration do not yet seem to be widely used options in settling divorce disputes – but they should be. These types of resolutions are relatively cheap, quick and painless when compared to courtroom clashes. The most suitable persons to mediate or arbitrate the parting of the ways are human rights lawyers, social workers or a trusted mutual friend.

Perhaps one day soon, marrying couples will learn from others' mistakes and wisely make provision in their marriage contracts for mandatory arbitration in the event of marital disputes, including divorce.

Even though two people know that the end of their marriage is near, it still comes as a shock to them when it happens. In a spiritual context, I believe that the 'life shock' of divorce is actually a 'gift' to those parting ways. This is because an irretrievable breakdown in a long-standing marriage forces the parties to re-examine many of the assumptions that have governed their day-to-day existence.

Separating partners need to extricate themselves from old patterns of behaviour that no longer serve their best interests. To reiterate what was written at the beginning of this 'conscious uncoupling' section, divorce offers a unique opportunity for couples to reinvent themselves; to fine-tune what makes them happy, and to discover new aspects of themselves that they had either forgotten about or never knew existed.

6

SUPER CHILDREN, SUPER PARENTS

Breaking the mould

Many couples are incredibly young and inexperienced when they take on the responsibility of raising children. Despite this, most of them do a great job, or the best they can, given their circumstances.

When we leave home and enter the big, wide world, we are essentially equipped with what our parents and schooling have taught us. It's really a backpack crammed quite untidily with smatterings of religion, stereotyping, prejudice, habits, relationships, a handful of skills, many untested thoughts, and maybe a piece of paper suggesting that we have done some studying.

With time, as we unpack our backpack along life's road, we notice something quite humbling: with the deepest of respect to our parents, we realise that what they offered us wasn't perfect, and that it had its limitations. In fact, the more we travel and experience what life has to offer, the more contained we recognise our upbringing actually was. Our parents showed us *a* way, which was the only way they knew how to do what is essentially the most difficult job in the world.

It was never our parents' intention to limit us. It's the last thing they would ever have deliberately wanted to do. As long as we can appreciate this, we can forever hold their efforts in our hearts.

> *Only once we recognise that we are prisoners of our own upbringing can we really plan our escape.*

At that moment of recognition, we can gently unhook that caravan of parental influence that we would otherwise have carted around with us for most of our lives. We can park that caravan and revisit it as and when we like – especially to relook at the good stuff for which we can be eternally grateful. But the secret in this life is to travel light, without a parental caravan in tow.

To evolve beyond our upbringing, we need to gently take our mothers and fathers off that parental pedestal where we rightly placed them in our youth. Again, with the utmost respect towards our parents, the sooner we do this, the quicker we can become our own person.

Breaking the mould of our upbringing is not done lightly, and probably not without some guilty discomfort. Kahlil Gibran's words are something of a tonic here when he writes: *"Pain is the breaking of the shell that encloses our understanding."*[15]

So, as parents, let's ponder the following:

> *We give children life; we never own them. We parent our children to give them wings, not to hold them back. We encourage our children to become authors of their own lives, not to follow in our own footsteps.*

A job for life

Behind every well-adjusted kid is a dedicated parent, and behind every dedicated parent is an unselfish commitment to leave this world a better place.

If done with the appropriate passion, commitment and selflessness, parenting must rank as one of the toughest and most underrated jobs in the world.

---

[15] Gibran, K. *The Prophet*, Studio Editions, 1995.

I have personally occupied some extremely demanding positions in my business career, yet none of them was as taxing or as rewarding as parenting. Many of the skills that I use in business today I learned from parenting.

The crazy fact about this most important job in the world is that nothing really prepares us for it. There was no Parenting 101 course in my day, and I'm not sure that it's yet on offer in any recognised learning institution. Would-be parents today are mostly left to fend for themselves by reading the latest and greatest books on parenting, speaking to others who have been through it, and then flying by the seat of their pants.

There is no magic formula for parenting. Raising children is far too complex for it to be that simple. I am, therefore, left to conclude the following:

> *There are as many ways to parent as there are creative minds to do the job.*

Parenting is a job for life. Regardless of the ripe old age that we and our children may reach, we still remain the parent.

The good news is that as newbie parents, we do actually have something of a head start. As mentioned, we can read the latest and greatest parenting books and talk to other parents, and of course, we have our default mode of parenting, which is how our parents brought us up. That may not necessarily be the ideal role model to adopt, but it is a way. Then there's instinct; that innate ability that is not to be underestimated. It comes from nowhere to give us a helping hand when we least expect it, but need it most. Finally, there's genetics – that 'nature' versus 'nurture' issue, where in a funny sort of way, we are working with semi-finished goods that have already been DNA-stamped.

The big picture of child rearing is this: our parenting opportunity is ostensibly a blank canvas on which we can create a beautiful work of art. What brushes, colours, paint types and textures we decide to use are up to us. But as with any artistic activity, there are basic guidelines that we would do well to follow. When drawing people, for example, one should get the body proportions right. My failed attempts at drawing portraits in my youth had my art teacher desperately pleading with me to "learn the damn fundamentals!"

The art of parenting is no different. I think there are fundamentals of which any aspiring parent should be aware. Rest assured, though: this chapter is *not* about listing "The Forty Fundamentals of Being a Great Parent". Who knows how many there are, and what they are? I simply want to raise a few of the more important issues that I came across while wearing the single parenting hat myself for a long time.

What I can assure you is that the birth of your child – even the handing over of that little adopted one in swaddling clothes – is an emotionally overwhelming event in your life. It cannot be compared to anything else. As 'mini-me' makes their grand entrance, nervousness evaporates into euphoria. That first little scream-cry of life in the labour ward tugs on your heartstrings, and it is a sound you will never forget. Dads, please make sure that you are there to witness it! After all, mom has endured a lot of hard labour to create a new life for you both; so at least be there to hand her that steaming package, fresh from the oven.

Nature is very tactical in how she softens the blow for new parents who are about to experience a complete change of lifestyle. It's a good thing that parents-to-be don't fully comprehend what's coming their way, otherwise they might be too easily distracted from the responsibility. Take heart, though:

all of the trials and tribulations that cross our parental paths are more than worth enduring. Parenting is nothing short of the finest character-building exercise for which we could ever volunteer. It offers us remarkable insights into life that can rarely be found in any other walk of life.

By the way, respect to those couples that make a conscious decision not to have children. A carefully considered choice is a far better course of action to take than an ill-conceived decision that could lead to a childhood of misery.

The crux of parenting

While studying for my teaching diploma year at university, the lecturers talked extensively about the formative years of a child's life. That is the 0-7 year old category, in which a child's final 'wiring' is soldered into place.

What children are exposed to at this early age forms the bedrock of their character. They are ultimately the sum of all their experiences: what they hear; what they see; what they do; what they learn; what they eat; and with whom they socialise – essentially everything to which they are exposed. They are like sponges that absorb absolutely all that is put in front of them. The interesting thing is that we don't realise this until it starts to manifest later.

If there is ever a time in our lives as parents when we need to invest a large *quantity and quality* of time with our offspring, this is it. There is no way around this, and unfortunately, it usually coincides with that time of life when parents have so many other distractions competing for their attention, like bedding down a marriage; settling into a new home; developing a circle of friends; managing the in-laws; dealing with big demands at the office; and getting all of the bills paid.

Try not to be one of those working parents who takes pride in telling everyone that they spend 30 minutes of quality time with their children every night, just before they go to bed. Sure, it's better than nothing, but it will likely have consequences later.

> *A missed parenting opportunity between the ages of 0-7 never returns. It's gone forever because that clock keeps ticking. Make the most of that window of opportunity before it closes on you.*

I can hear some of you protesting that a full-time mother, father, well-qualified *au pair*, or grandparent could make up for some lost ground here. I take your point, but all I am proposing is that Mom and Dad bring their A-game to the table – all the more so if they have full-time jobs. If, as parents, we end up skimping on these golden, formative years with our children, then spare a moment for the following cartoon.

"I skimped a little on the foundation, but no one'll ever know it."

Parenting is a selfless act. As adults, we have to deprioritise our own needs and address the needs of our children first. This is a very tough discipline to instil because we are so used to having all of our time to ourselves. Read the above three sentences again to make sure that the penny has dropped.

Being there through each stage

During their waking hours in particular, babies need our physical presence for their own safety. It's a very vulnerable period for the parent and the child – one mistake and we can pay a high price. But don't stress about this, just be aware of it. Our parental instincts normally do a good job in protecting us during this phase, despite how tired we may be.

As our babies start crawling and interacting with us, our minds will often be tempted to drift elsewhere. We may be there with our child physically, but our minds will want to wander off and do something a little less mind-numbing, like texting, working on a computer, reading a magazine, or just tapping out and daydreaming about something in the distant recesses of our minds.

As alluring as it may be to divide our attention and multi-task between what our baby needs from us versus what our minds want from us, it's a dangerous conflict of interest to entertain. It leads to a dilution of focus that can end up with the parent doing a well-below-average job on both fronts.

As babies develop into toddlers and beyond, they become naturally more curious about life. We really want to nurture this zest for life, because it's how they learn the workings of this world. When we get down to their level and climb into their minds, we can figure out more easily just where they're at. For some parents, this may mean switching from a work office environment down to a Lego-spattered carpet within minutes of getting home. This requires switching mental gears from one extreme to another, and it can be a big ask of a tired parent at the end of a day. However, when we are in the moment with our explorative toddlers, that is when we are able to identify and reinforce their interests. It is also how we build valuable emotional bonds with them. At this stage of our child's life, being fully present really is our gift to them.

In one moment, we can find ourselves answering a barrage of questions from our toddler, whose retort to many of our answers can repeatedly – and sometimes irritatingly – be: "But why?" In the next moment, we can be yanking our little one physically out of harm's way. Not surprisingly, we develop eyes in the back of our heads, because naïve curiosity has no sense of danger.

Importantly, never underestimate how much toddlers absorb things before being able to verbalise them. It can come as quite a shock when toddlers suddenly repeat their parents' expletives with gay abandon in front of others.

It is easier to just accept that for about the first seven years of rearing a child, time is no longer our own. It's on the backburner. There's no denying it, parenting is a relentless task; it's the great leveller. It's the greatest time sacrifice we will ever need to make in our lives, because time is our scarcest resource. But commitment, planning and spousal support can get us comfortably through it.

I am also confident in advocating that it will be the best seven-year investment that you will ever make in your entire life. This is the crux of parenting.

The gift of self-esteem

It is often said that the greatest gift that we can develop in our children is a strong self-esteem. We should try to equip our children with the confidence to be comfortable in their own skin, self-assured in what they do with their lives, and in possession of a healthy dose of self-respect.

But, as a parent, how does one foster this? Each of us has something that we are good at; it's just a case of finding it, nurturing it, and chain-reacting it until it becomes a centre of excellence in our children's lives. It really helps for parents to be aware of what excites their children, because that natural spark of interest is often where they end up excelling. To be able to spot a particular talent in our children, we need to be sufficiently in tune with them to make the discovery along with them.

It doesn't have to be something that our child will necessarily end up doing as a profession; it can be a transient interest, like building models, which could lead to an interest in the construction business; or flying radio-controlled planes, which could lead to an interest in the aviation industry.

Importantly, it must be something that the child loves doing, not what the parent wants the child to do. Too often parents want to relive their lives vicariously through their offspring. That's a parenting mistake that can come at a high price.

Trying to nurture self-esteem in our child could be explored along the following lines: once our child latches on to something that they really enjoy, there's a high chance that they will become good at it. When they become good at it, they gain confidence. Their talent then becomes evident to onlookers, who start admiring and respecting the child for what they can do. This affirmation in turn boosts the child's self-esteem further and starts to give purpose and meaning to their life. It's a chain reaction that once started, feeds on itself and builds a momentum all of its own. This can have a profound influence on the rest of the child's life.

Think about this too: once children engage with something that preoccupies their minds, we, as parents, don't have to sit there and continuously entertain them. We are giving them wings to fly.

⋄⋄⋄

From an early age, my two boys loved using their hands to build things. It started with basic Lego blocks, and graduated to a composite set of Technic Lego that contained fibre optics, mechanically moving parts, and electronic bits and pieces. That brought the whole construction game alive for them.

By the age of around seven, my sons were building things that I, as an adult, couldn't have dreamed of building myself. They then graduated to buying pre-packed electronic kits to build radios, alarms and the like. After that, they started tinkering with desktop computers. It was not long before they were pulling two computers apart and building a superior machine with spare parts and upgraded motherboards. They then started making their own motherboards – all self-taught via the internet. Eventually, my older son graduated as a computer scientist, and my younger son as an electro-mechanical engineer.

⋄⋄⋄

We need to find whatever it is that interests our children, and then repeatedly bait the hook to suit the fish. If they run with it, then as parents we will know that we are on to something significant. If it gets real traction, they will start learning far more on their own than we could ever have hoped to teach them ourselves. And bingo! That's the moment in which their journeys start.

This leads me to a side note: parenting used to be a one-way teaching street. The adult always knew better, and the children always remained the students until they left home. In these modern technological times, this has been turned somewhat on its head and has blown a breath of fresh air into the traditional parent-child relationship.

Whenever we spot a chance to let our children teach us something, we should take it with both hands. Opportunities shouldn't be difficult to find these days, considering how tech-savvy our children are, compared to us, as parents. I was continuously amazed at what my children were able to teach me from a very young age. I'm prepared to put my head on a block that it was a real morale booster for them, too.

The emotional credit system

Every kind act on the part of a parent towards their child is an emotional credit banked in the child's mind account.

The greater the number of emotional credits we bank with our children, the easier our relationship with them becomes. These transactions happen mostly at a subconscious level, but as a responsible parent, it's very useful to know that this dynamic exists.

Here's the interesting thing about this concept: when we have banked many emotional credits with our children, we may suddenly need to debit the account by doing or saying something they don't particularly want or like, but which is necessary. However, due to the many emotional credits already banked, the children are usually more than happy to go along with it, without complaint. This plays out more strongly as children grow older.

⊰·⊱

My boys loved exploring a nearby forest. They used to trawl the rivers for the likes of tadpoles, crabs and fish. They also explored under rocks and logs, in search of scorpions, snakes, spiders and a whole host of insect life. On one of many occasions, they asked me to take them to the forest, where they made two discoveries that day.

The first was a large bank of clay next to the river. At first, they gingerly gouged out handfuls of yellow, pink and beige clays. They then squelched them together dipping their mix into the river to make the clay more malleable. I was surprised at how dexterous they quickly became in sculpting all sorts of interesting objects, and I made sure to let them know how much I admired their efforts. I'll never forget how proud the sculptors were that day.

On our walk down from the river, my elder son made another discovery: he turned over a rock and found a clutch of small white stones that looked like peppermint sweets. Intrigued, he slipped a couple of them into his pocket. Well, imagine our surprise when, on our way home, squeals of delight came from the back seat of the car as my son produced a baby gecko that had hatched right there and then in his pocket!

⊰·⊱

The point of these two stories is this: when we do for our children what they want to do, they really appreciate us for it. If we can have fun in the process as well, they appreciate us even more. On top of that, if we end up praising them for a job well done, then we take their experience to a whole new level. How can we not endear ourselves, or bank emotional credits, with our children when we make time to do things like this with them?

THE LADDER OF LIFE: BALANCING THE CLIMB

I'm not for one minute suggesting that we need to employ a deliberate tactic to score brownie points with our children; it's simply a process whereby children, by osmosis, emotionally bank meaningful experiences with those parents who take the trouble to spend quality time with them.

So, when I got home after an outing like that with my boys, and I asked them to jump into their baths, they did so without complaint. After bathing, if I asked them to start tidying their rooms and tackling their homework before dinner, they did so willingly. If I needed some help in the kitchen, they jumped in to help me. It's a natural exchange of emotional debits and credits that never consciously occurred in the heads of either boy.

Parents who do not get willing co-operation from their children probably have two things at play. Firstly, the parent is unlikely to have been making the minimum of effort with the children to be able to bank sufficient emotional credits with them. Secondly, the parent has probably been more demanding of the children than could reasonably have been expected of them, thereby further depleting any remaining emotional credits. When credits run dry, the children's co-operation peters out. And when they run super-dry, defiance sets in. That's often the start of disciplinary issues between parent and child.

> *It's a natural law of life: if you give a lot of yourself to others in this life, the universe at some stage willingly gives it back to you, with interest.*

Life just operates this way, and there's no more rewarding way to discover this than through your own children.

If you're vaguely sceptical about what I'm saying here, observe which parent the children physically gravitate towards in the event of a crisis. It's invariably the parent who has banked the most emotional credits with them. But remember, it's not a competition between the parents as to who can bag the most emotional credits. It's simply about both parents investing plenty of quality time with their children, especially in their formative years.

Raising the mirror

The old cliché goes: "The apple does not fall far from the tree." In other words, our children's behaviour very much reflects our own behaviour, as parents.

In their formative years, children are essentially a carbon copy of their parents. Everything we do and say as parents is mimicked by our children. After all, we are by far their most significant teachers, so why wouldn't they learn primarily from us? Because children replicate much of what we say and do as parents in their early years, we have to be extremely careful about what we say and do in front of them.

> *As we raise our children, so we raise the mirror in front of ourselves. If we don't like what we see, we need to change ourselves.*

This is a hard-hitting statement to make, but it's true. The sooner we back off from trying to blame our children for everything, the better. Bear in mind that when we blame our children, we are indirectly accusing ourselves.

An adapted version of the Serenity Prayer essentially says the same thing:

"God, grant me the serenity to accept the people
  I cannot change,
The courage to change the ones that I can,
And the wisdom to know it's me."

To minimise having to continuously remedy our own behaviour as a parent, I recommend that parents pay close attention to three core values around the house. They are the magic ingredients of a happy home. If we shoot straight with these three values from the get-go, we'll make life a whole lot easier for ourselves as parents.

The three core values are:

1. Respect
2. Consistency
3. Fairness.

Let's put each one under the microscope quickly to get a feel for how powerful they are.

Respect

It is a fundamental principle to treat everybody in this life with equal respect. Whether we are talking to a domestic worker, garbage collector, prime minister, or our own child, they are all deserving of the same respect. Whether we are talking to a man or a woman, a white person or a black person, someone else's child or our own child, we should do so with the utmost respect. There is never a reason to talk to our child in a puerile, condescending or overly authoritarian manner.

If, as parents, we show a healthy respect towards our children's rights, privacy, possessions, emotions, friends and dreams, then we're putting our relationship with them on a solid footing. There is no reason to ever belittle, make fun of, or disrespect any aspect of our children's' lives – even if we think we're being humorous in the process.

Shouting at our children should be an anathema for parents as well – with the only exception being if their lives are in immediate danger. Would we ever shout at our local preacher, our boss at work, or even ourselves? Obviously not. So why would we then shout at our children? A loving relationship between parent and child requires great sensitivity; and part of being sensitive is avoiding the need to shout-communicate at our children.

If, as a parent, we are angry, it is preferable to be quietly assertive rather than loudly aggressive towards our children.

Importantly, our use of language in front of our children says a lot about the level of respect that exists between family members. If we refer to our children as the "brats", "rug-rats", or some other derogatory term, we're unlikely to endear ourselves to them. If we go as far as to suggest to their faces that they are "clumsy" or "useless" at something, I believe that we are making a rod for our own backs. Children absorb everything that we say, and it can directly impact on their self-esteem. They are not only able to store every disparaging remark that we make about them; they are also able to retrieve them at will in circumstances that are unlikely to be to our advantage. Regardless of our type of sense of humour, is it really worth talking about our children like this?

Let me finish on the topic of respect with the following true story.

❦

A schoolteacher was standing in for another teacher who went on leave. While researching some facts about the students he was going to teach, he noticed that one particular class had an unusually high set of IQ scores, ranging from 120-145.

The teacher decided to treat this particular class with the utmost respect. He got to know every pupil by his or her first name; he continuously monitored their progress; and he ensured that they all remained academically challenged. His expectations of that class grew with every day that passed, and his rapport with them was outstanding. As a consequence, those students produced stunning results.

The principal was so impressed that he called in the relief teacher to enquire how he had pulled it off, especially since that class was not considered particularly bright – in fact, quite the contrary. The surprised teacher claimed that he had been dealing with very intelligent children, and that the results could have been expected. He then showed the principal their IQ scores.

The principal was taken aback and immediately pointed out that the 'IQ scores' were in fact the children's locker numbers!

❦

Consistency

Children draw immense security from their relationships with a parent who shows great consistency in their emotional temperament. This allows children to anticipate how a parent will react in a certain scenario. If a child can anticipate how a parent will respond, they can draw clear boundaries in their lives, and by inference, with other people too.

Of course, it helps tremendously if the parent is consistently pleasant towards their offspring. That frees up everyone in the family to get on constructively with their lives.

My own mother was an alcoholic for 40 years. Her drinking habits started when I was about five years old, so I learned first-hand what it was like to try to emotionally connect with a parent who was inebriated on a daily basis. It was impossible. The parent who grapples with an addiction blows hot and cold towards all of those around them, and it's a recipe for erratic relationships and protracted emotional pain.

In such a situation, the child eventually reaches a point where they can no longer deal with the inconsistency of it all, and they respond by holding that parent at an emotional arm's length. They believe that by not getting too close, they can't get hurt. Anything that creates distance between the parent and child should be removed as quickly as possible. It's horribly detrimental to the relationship.

The same can be said of the child who has a parent with no interest in controlling their mood swings. For a child to have to walk on eggshells around a moody parent – wondering whether or not they are going to have their head bitten off if they say or do the wrong thing – is supremely selfish behaviour on the part of the moody parent.

When children are subjected to this kind of treatment by their parents, they can, in acute cases, retreat into the safe haven of their own ethereal worlds. As a result, they can develop reclusive and uncommunicative personalities that stay with them for life.

Perhaps one of the more notorious examples of inconsistency is when a parent promises something to a child, and then fails to deliver on that promise. If parents knew the anguish and disappointment to which they subject their child every time they do this, they would never break their promises. In not keeping to our word as parents, we strike at the very heart of issues such as trust, reliability and responsibility, which negatively impact our relationship with our children, and ultimately, their relationships with others.

The golden rule is never to promise something to our children that we may not be able to deliver. If we think we can deliver on our promise, then rather under-promise and over-deliver. It's much kinder on everybody that way.

Fairness

It is uncanny, but children instinctively know when you, as a parent, are being unfair. Perhaps it's a sixth sense. Maybe children are far more astute at reading body language than that for which we adults give them credit. Children can just smell when their parents are being unfair or unreasonable.

For example, when we shut down a robust debate on what our children consider to be a very important issue – and we do so using that conversation-killer-blow: "Because I said so!" we are starting World War III.

Imagine a fly on the wall observing us, as parents, pulling that stunt. I think the fly would, in no uncertain terms, tell us the following: firstly, we pulled rank as the adult. By shutting down the discussion, we also implied that we knew better than the child. Secondly, in squashing the dialogue, we extinguished the possibility of our children learning the art of debate, reasoning, logic and compromise. Thirdly, we overlooked the fact that children are enormously logical. Their logic may not always be correct; but it's our job in the moment to point out why their thinking is irrational. The only way we can do that is by keeping the conversation alive. Fourthly, if we believe that adults are always right, we need to recalibrate our thinking. For some bizarre reason, there are parents out there who think they have to be right all of the time. Those parents are often the types to shut down conversation as soon as they realise that they're on the wrong side of the argument. Many children can see right through such aberrant behaviour.

If we do a postmortem on a contentious argument between ourselves and our children that ended up in tears, in nine cases out of ten, we will most likely find a legitimate reason why our children challenged the status quo in the first place. For example, we may have misheard what our child actually said. Perhaps we did not realise the double standard we were inadvertently creating by, for example, finding fault with one child only when in fact both children were guilty of the same thing.

Instead of feeling threatened, let's rather be delighted that our child has the courage and conviction to challenge us on something – as long as they do so respectfully. We can teach them how to be respectful if they don't yet have that skill. Children may not be right much of the time, but they are certainly not wrong all of the time either.

> *Blessed is the parent who can openly admit to the error of their ways, for this is how the child, too, learns the art of apologising to others.*

Choice of schooling

Once children are beyond the age of seven, it is strategic of parents to deliberately shift more of the responsibility for their children's upbringing to the schools they will be attending.

Apart from school holidays, our children will spend, on average, eight hours every day at school. If we consider that they sleep for another eight hours every day, then up to half of their waking life can be spent at school. It is no wonder then that, for children, their school can be likened to their 'other home'; their teachers to their 'other parents'; and their classmates to their 'other siblings'.

Our children only have one school career. They only have one crack at the opportunity, and then it's done. In addition to this, schooling happens when they are at their most impressionable age, so their school experience will stay with them forever. For these reasons, the choice of schooling for our children is absolutely critical for their happiness, growth and development.

If we disliked school ourselves, then we might be biased in our decision towards which type of learning institution would best suit our child. If this is the case, we need to involve others in the decision, including our child, but only if they are old enough to contribute to the discussion.

> *After all, children who are consulted are more committed to a decision that includes their opinion.*

There can be no question about the deep impact that the school experience will have on our children's lives. Here are a few thoughts perhaps worth considering before making the schooling decision.

- Tradition can paralyse our thinking. What worked well for us when we were at school decades ago may well not work for our children today. Because we had a great time at a particular school does not necessarily mean that our child is going to thrive in the same set-up. Trying to reheat the soufflé doesn't really work. Besides, schools go through good cycles and bad cycles, which is largely dependent on the quality of the individual heading up the institution.
- There are different schools for different personalities. Since our offspring are often wildly different from one another, it makes sense not to herd them all into the same learning institution. One size does not necessarily fit all. As inconvenient as this may be from the family-taxi point of view, this is not about the parents' expedience, but about the child's experience.
- If you believe that the purpose of a good education is to prepare your child for life, then a co-educational opportunity is probably the better option. This world is almost 50% male and 50% female, so your child needs to get along with both sexes from an early age. I have seen too many people's lives being derailed by their inability to cope socially with what's waiting for them out there beyond the school's gates.
- Without wanting to promote any form of elitism, private schooling may well be worth considering for your particular child. The classes are generally smaller, and they can attract better quality teachers because they pay them more. Their facilities are also usually superior to those of government schools. It would also seem that private-school alumni usually have stronger *alma mater* networks from which they can benefit in their later years. However, there can be great government school options, too, so do the research on the institution that would best suit your child.

- A school's local community and parent body can offer invaluable input regarding the 'goings-on' at a particular school. Asking the principal to share his educational philosophies with you face-to-face can be very revealing. Even a walk around the school grounds while the school is operationally in full swing can certainly give you a better 'feel' for the establishment.

Choosing the 'right' school for our children is an enormously important decision. If we get it wrong, or things change unexpectedly, it is vital not to just let our children grin and bear unpleasant circumstances. It could be opportune to change schools if our child develops a significant talent for playing a musical instrument, but their school has no music department; or we discover that our child happens to be saddled with a particularly poor vintage that includes some unsavoury characters in their class. Or Mom and Dad may decide to get divorced, in which case reassessed financial resources usually dictate a new order. Staying agile is important. If it is right to move our child to another school, then so be it. However, moving our child continuously from one school to another can be very disruptive and counter-productive to their development. That, too, is best avoided.

> *It is said that a parent is as happy as their saddest child.*

We therefore owe it to ourselves as parents to ensure that our children have happy schooling experiences. It can set the tone for the rest of their lives, including our lives as the parents.

Afterthoughts on parenting

Children learn far more by what we *do* as parents than by what we *say*. We are their walking role models, so let's put our best foot forward at all times and seek to influence them positively, every step of the way. It will pay handsome dividends in the end.

Children can preoccupy themselves with an activity and become incredibly absorbed and content with what they are doing. As parents, we may be tempted to muscle in on the action, thinking that perhaps we can make it more interesting or more fun for them. My advice is this: don't try to make a happy child happier. It is unwise to disturb contentment in our children. Rather just let them continue concentrating on what they're doing. Besides, one of the goals of parenting is to encourage independence in our children's thinking and actions.

Don't be afraid to firmly discipline children when it's called for. Children can literally scream for parental guidance. Help children draw boundaries for themselves, because no learning or loving can take place unless it is anchored in generous amounts of structure and routine. As any good teacher will tell you, it is better to start with our hands firmly on the reins, and then loosen our grip over time. Trying to do it the other way round doesn't really work very well. How we discipline our children is our call, but as our understanding of this topic has evolved over time, it is now commonly understood that the slapped child becomes the parent who slaps. We therefore need to modernise our approach.

Those parents who are a little obsessive about the tidiness of their homes can often find themselves saying to their little ones: "Don't do this," and "Don't do that," and "Watch out for this," and "Do be careful with that." Instead of constantly preventing our toddlers from doing what is normal to them, rather distract them with a substitute with which they can fiddle. Pulling out all of the plastic containers, pots, pans and wooden spoons from the kitchen drawers can be a safe and beautifully noisy distraction for them. This positive distraction tactic can be deployed anywhere in the home without causing any real damage. It is better to apply our minds and find alternative entertainment for our children than to simply defend the house as if it were a museum.

Children thrive in other children's company. For them to have a number of 'besties' in their youth is a vital ingredient to becoming a well-adjusted adult. Be on the look-out for playmates for your children – just ensure that there is effective adult supervision when your child is playing with others. Bullying is more prevalent than we think, and it can forever stain a child's memory. You don't want any hanky-panky going on, either.

An interesting life belongs to those with curious minds. The secret is to find things to do with our children that will pique their interest and curiosity. If we can nurture a vivid imagination in our children by, for example, telling them some of our own home-baked bedtime stories, it can spark tremendous creativity within them. Curiosity, imagination and creativity ignite original thinking, which is an asset worth encouraging in every youngster today.

One of the greatest gifts we can give our children is a love for reading: it is the source of much wisdom. What's more, our children can get endless pleasure from this activity throughout their entire lives. For youngsters, reading is also a healthy distraction from any unsavoury mischief that might tempt them in moments of boredom. If we're struggling to get their interest in reading kickstarted, finding an article on a topic that they really love, no matter how juvenile it may seem, could help.

Avoid talking to your spouse through the child. For example, when Daddy says to little Olivia: "Your mommy is going to look after you and prepare lunch while I go off and play golf now, isn't she?" he is making Olivia the ham in the sandwich. The child will soon wise up when Mommy expresses her unhappiness after Daddy disappears out the front door with his golf bag in tow.

The world has changed so much since I was first a parent, and I don't think it has become an easier or safer place. I do not pretend to know or understand half of the challenges that parents have to deal with today, but I would suggest that parents enlighten their children (when the time seems right) about the 'temptation hooks' of life that can snag and drag them down. The consequences of indulging unsafely in the likes of booze, drugs, sex, gambling and the dark web need to be made very clear to our children. Too much of a 'good thing' at too young an age can actually be a very bad thing in the long run.

Wise parents adjust their parenting style to each of their children *and* as their children get older. As my younger son once said to me: "Parenting should not just be a matter of rinse and repeat." As a parent, it may be very tempting to take the easier route and to continue doing what we've always done – but our previous methods are often no longer appropriate or effective. Our children appreciate us staying current and relevant for them for as long as we can.

Grandparents can be a truly wonderful influence on their grandchildren. They have earned their parenting stripes, and like all of us, are usually much better at doing things second time round. It would be prudent, therefore, to give our children as much exposure as possible to their grandparents. However, be considerate when making use of grandparents' contributions.

I recall a grandmother unambiguously reminding her daughter that she was the "granny, not the nanny".

This chapter has emphasised the importance of investing time in the development of our children. Unsurprisingly, a very pleasant discovery down life's road is that our grandchildren turn out to be the interest on that investment.

7

DONNING OUR SPIRITUAL ARMOUR

Religious beginnings

◆◆◆

I attended an Anglican church school for 11 years. Religious assemblies were a daily ritual at our school chapel, and attendance was compulsory.

It was a routine into which I slipped quite comfortably and without much thought. Being involved in a values-based and community-orientated activity seemed like a good idea at the time and there was really no need to question it.

Looking back, *my religion was unapologetic about being exclusive*. The Jewish boys did not attend our services, and went elsewhere for their prayers.

My religion was most certainly traditional. It was the way, the truth and the life, based on the experiences of those who had walked thousands of years before us. It was a tried and tested formula that was supposedly tailored to our spiritual wellbeing.

My religion was also book-based. There was the Bible, which is as ancient as the hills; then there were the service books, which we never bothered to open, because we knew the order of the service off by heart – including the priest's wording. Lastly, there were the hymn books and psalm books that never once changed in all of the years I was there. They're probably still there. As a choir boy, singing brought me some light relief from the seriousness of it all.

Finally, *my religion was ritualistic.* All church services were more or less at the same time of day, in the same format, of the same length, with the same priest, and with more or less the same wording and events. Some of the schoolboys got into the habit of listening to every word that came out of the preacher's mouth, in case he made a mistake. For mischievous teenagers, that was something of a highlight in a service.

Our Christian education did offer something of a promise. The priest, who was unquestionably a man of God, maintained that if we observed all of the major religious days, followed

Biblical advice, and attended church regularly, we would be reasonably assured of a good life. One was left to surmise that if we continued to follow these rules in our lives, the remote control to the Pearly Gates would most likely be within our reach.

Some years after I left school, history began to fascinate me. There was an enormous amount of catching up to do, because it was not a subject I had taken at school. My findings on religious matters were intriguing, to say the least. I had never heard of religions such as Taoism, Confucianism, Jainism, Shinto, Sikhism and Zoroastrianism, which had hundreds of millions of global worshippers, particularly in the East.

Neither was I aware that all of the major religions of this world, namely Buddhism, Christianity, Islam, Hinduism and Judaism had their own 'mystical teachings'. Surprisingly, these teachings are all remarkably similar to one another. They essentially refer to the route that mystics take in seeking the truth: that personal, inward journey that reveals a spiritual reality hidden from our normal awareness.

These mystical teachings fascinated me and were a refreshing change from the rather bland religious diet that had been served up at school. As I delved further into the history books, I learned that new religions are being spawned all of the time. They start as movements or cults, and if they amass a sufficient following, they become established as a recognised religion. Many such cults have fallen by the wayside – some quite infamously, largely due to the hypocritical conduct of their charismatic, evangelical leaders.

❧

I suppose like all things man-made, religion has attracted its fair share of controversy. While a plethora of 'good books' have been crafted to offer religious seekers prescriptions for righteous living, the interpretation of these religious scripts has really thrown the cat among the pigeons in modern times.

Religious fanatics – people who double their efforts but lose sight of the aim – have started many wars through the ages, with too many lives having been lost in the name of religion. Some of today's religious fanatics are still sacrificing themselves with horrific brutality and are willing to kill even innocent bystanders. Not surprisingly, critics throughout history have been quick to label most forms of religious activity as widespread indoctrination – the *"opium of the people"*[16], as Karl Marx once put it.

I will be the first to acknowledge that billions of people have derived much comfort from being deeply religious, but we do need to bear in mind that most of them cannot be religious without being largely exclusive in their practices.

The more I researched the topic of religion, the more questions it raised for me. It was with some relief that I stumbled across the writings of a spiritual guru who shared this wisdom with the world: *"All the great religions are like the great rivers of this earth; they all flow to the one great ocean of Truth."*[17]

This made a lot of sense to me, and it again brought into focus the question of why religions had to be exclusive in their approach, when in fact they were all heading towards the same goal. Their single goal is surely to reconnect people to God, the Divine Creator, the One Source, a Higher Power – whatever one would like to call it.

This maxim gracefully encapsulated for me the idea that each religion offers *a* way of getting us to the Universal Truth. Regardless of which spiritual route we take, all roads ultimately lead to the same destination.

---

16 Marx, K. *A Contribution to the Critique of Hegel's Philosophy of Right*, 1843.
17 Freke, T. and Gandy, P. *World Mysticism*, Judy Piatkus,1997.

This is also when I recognised the fork in the road: we can either take the orthodox religious approach, in which someone authoritative instructs us from a pulpit how to get there in a communally organised way; or we can go within ourselves and find the truth lying in the deep recesses of our own minds – just as the mystics of all religions have done through the centuries.

Now that I was starting to see the bigger picture unfolding in front of me, it was hard to believe that there had been this choice all along. Life thereafter became much more interesting.

Chance discovery

About 15 years after I left school, I received a phone call from a good friend out of the blue. With great excitement in his voice, he was insistent that I sign up for a course with him. It was to be a week-long experience with some Americans from the Light Institute in Galisteo, New Mexico. He garbled something to the effect that they were New-Age people offering a new-fangled technique for exploring our inner-self: something called 'life regression'.

I nearly dropped the cordless phone in my bubble bath. Had I heard right? Life regression? What on Earth was that? My friend tried again to explain it to me, but I don't really think he knew either. Despite the steep cost of the course, and the fact that I was none the wiser about what it was all about, I signed up. I trusted my friend's judgment.

> *I convinced myself that there was nothing to lose by taking a walk on the wild side – as long as it wasn't life threatening.*

I had one last chance to question my decision when I found myself lying naked under a duvet in front of a strange woman who was waving a light box above my bed. After she had applied some light and acupressure to certain parts of my cranium, and gently talked me down into a safe space, my journey began.

A great deal happened during those five days. My first experience was quite an unexpected and dramatic 'communication' with my deceased grandmother. A large amount of information suddenly swept through my mind in what seemed like an instantaneous download of factual and emotional information from who-knows-where? It was a message that meant a lot to me, but it immediately brought me to tears. I had not really grieved since her passing 20 years earlier, and for all intents and purposes, she had been my surrogate mother for the first 18 years of my life.

During that week of 'life regression', I also chanced on tapping into what the Easterners affectionately refer to as "prana", a universal energy that is supposedly available to us all. I 'patternised' this prana through my hands in what were, according to the life regression facilitator, standard Reiki movements. Back then, I had never heard of Reiki, let alone how to spell it. That energy also enabled me to sense and give attention to my solar plexus chakra, which I happened to stumble across.

I was also able to recall seven of my 'previous lives' in great detail: from being a wheeltapper on the French railways to being an English concert pianist. Every life had significance in relation to the one I am living today.

Most importantly, during those five days, I learned to quickly still my mind. At a later stage, that would become a gateway to accessing much of what I had been exposed to during that 'life regression' week, and more.

By the end of the five days, I was exhausted and shell-shocked by the experience. But I was also exhilarated by the possibilities that lay before me. I had to ask myself why, at the age of 34, was I only then discovering how little I knew about my own mind and body. What was all of this latent potential; this mystery lurking just behind the thin veil of one's own perception?

To say that the life regression experience turned my life upside down would be the understatement of the century. Never before had I discovered a part of myself that I never knew existed; something that is accessible through very specific mind-body techniques and available to us all. The best way to analogise the experience is to explain it via a dream that I had shortly after taking part in that course.

> *I was living in a spacious house in the English countryside. It was a beautifully decorated home in which I had lived for many years. One day, I was absolutely astonished to discover a door in the house that I had never noticed before.*
>
> *Intrigued with this discovery, I opened the door to find a large and magnificently furnished bedroom. Everything was covered in a thin coat of dust, indicating that that area of the house had been undiscovered and out of commission for some time. I threw open the curtains, and a large window afforded a unique vista of the garden. It was an angle from which I had never before had the privilege of seeing the garden. It was all quite overwhelming, so I sat down on the dusty bed, dumbfounded that the room had been right under my nose for all those years without my ever realising it.*

I worked out long before that particular dream that my house symbolises my body in my dreams. Being surprised at stumbling across that room was the equivalent of being startled by a discovery of a part of my mind-body that I never knew existed. The fact that the room was dusty suggested that that part of my mind had not been used for a long time. When I opened the curtains to the view of the garden, I likened it to my opening up my awareness (during the life regression), which gave me another view on life.

I finished the one-on-one life regression programme with more questions than answers: how did that communication with my grandmother work? What was that vibrant energy channelling through my hands, and where did it come from?

Did we all have access to it, and was it a type of healing force, perhaps? Were those all really past lives that I had seen, because they seemed so detailed and real? Did this make reincarnation a real possibility? Who had formulated the insightful lessons from each one of my past lives that were perfectly tailored to help me in my current life? I knew that I, myself, had verbalised the lessons from these lives – not the facilitator accompanying me – but where had all of that information come from?

I had too many question, and simply too few answers.

Stilling the mind

It took me a long time before I could access that energy flow in my hands again. I had to learn, through my own self-taught meditation, how to recreate the circumstances under which it would return – and boy, was I happy to get it back!

Although the sensation of this energy was intoxicating, the more important issue at hand was putting it to good use. With time, I learned more about how to do that; but this falls outside the scope of this book.

The power of meditation

Over time, I discovered that using meditation to go within myself enabled me to find remedies to my physical, emotional, mental and spiritual wellbeing. I believe meditation to be a kind of preventative medicine that is literally available at our fingertips, whenever and wherever we need it. No special skill or licence is needed to meditate – anyone can do it. Only two proficiencies are required: discipline and persistence.

The art of meditating is to increase the gaps between our thoughts until we have no more thoughts moving through our mind. When we find that silent gap between our thoughts, we rest in that blissful state of 'nothingness'. It is where one learns to just 'be'.

Completely draining our mental swamp to reach a state of 'nothingness' is what meditation is all about. But the more preoccupied our minds are, the more persistent and disciplined we need to be to empty them. It is for this reason that finding that state of nothingness during a meditation can be quite an elusive exercise, especially for those starting out.

Paradoxically though, it is only when we finally reach that place where we no longer have a single thought left in our minds – that state of nothingness – that we have sensory access to previously unrealised facets of our entire being. I believe that we are spiritual beings having an occasional human experience, not human beings having an occasional spiritual experience. Regularly finding ways to 'plug into source' is therefore essential, comforting and energising.

So, where do we start?

A good place to start meditating is *understanding the geography of our minds*. Buddhist tradition suggests that we have many minds, but two are of particular interest here.

The primordial mind

This mind is as old as the ages, infinite in its depth and abundant in its calmness. It is unchanging, clear, bright and radiant. It is devoid of any emotion and free from any thought. It is the 'nothing' that is the natural opposite of 'everything' that normally goes on inside our heads.

The ordinary mind

This mind contains all of the audio and movie tapes that play relentlessly in our heads. It is the mind that plots and plans, manipulates and controls. It is a slave to habit and continually craves things. It is also where the emotional wrecking ball lets loose. It is a shallow, restless mind, littered with many illusions and much busyness and noise.

We can compare these two minds when we look carefully into a pond of water. When the water is very still, we can see with great clarity into it: from the tadpoles, fish and crabs down to the detailed patterns on the mud at the bottom of the pond. That is the clarity of the still, primordial mind. But when we put our hands into the pond and agitate the water, it stirs up a cloud of mud that totally obscures everything from our vision. That is the obfuscation of the agitated, ordinary mind.

When meditating, the skill is to *slip quietly from our ordinary minds into our primordial minds*. If we can do this regularly and to great effect, we may be pleasantly surprised at what we find.

If you wish to meditate:
- Find a quiet place, preferably at dawn or dusk, where you will not be disturbed for about an hour.
- Choose a lighter rather than darker place to meditate.
- Take off all of your metal jewellery.
- Find a comfortable position in which you can keep your back as straight as a pin. If you have the ability to sit comfortably with a straight back – either on a chair, or in the lotus position – then do so. Otherwise, lie down on your back, with your legs extended straight out and flat on the ground, with your feet slightly apart.

- Place your arms gently down by your sides on the floor, or alongside each other, palms down, across the top of your solar plexus area.
- Do not cross your arms or legs at any stage of your meditation.
- It is not recommended that you lie on your bed as you will likely fall asleep. This would defeat the purpose. Meditating is *not* sleeping; it is stilling your mind yet remaining in a very mentally alert state.
- Do not eat a full meal just before meditating; and ensure that you are not under the influence of alcohol or any other mind-altering substance. If you are to benefit from the escape, your body and mind must be clean and clear.
- Focus on your breathing – the passageway that will lead you to the door of your primordial mind. Bring your attention to the air flowing in and out of your nostrils. Find a rhythm of inhaling and exhaling in equal lengths, all the while listening to your breath. Concentrate on the rush of air over your upper lip.
- Still your mind further, and then slow down your thoughts, again increasing the gap between your thoughts.
- Don't engage in any of your thoughts. Just observe them. Let them pass through. Constantly seek to increase that gap between your thoughts, until you have no more thoughts left in your head.
- Keep your breathing regular. This could take up to half an hour, but don't ever watch a clock. Just focus on your breathing and on emptying your mind.

An effective meditation has physiological effects on your body, too: your heart rate slows down; your blood pressure drops;

your metabolism decreases; your muscles noticeably relax; and your brain waves morph from a beta to an alpha rhythm. During a powerful meditation experience, you will also feel your body temperature dropping, so make sure that you are sufficiently warmly dressed before you start.

If you are new to meditation, you may find that after about 15 minutes, your body starts responding in noticeable ways. Your body may jerk suddenly, and on more than one occasion. You may sometimes also feel hot patches swimming around in parts of your body. Just observe them; there's no need to worry about them or to try to control them. If you get itchy somewhere, feel free to scratch. You don't want any lingering distractions.

At all times, stay focused on your rhythmical breathing and on emptying your mind. You might well find that after a couple of weeks of dedicated daily effort, the technique of stilling your mind comes more easily to you, and the benefits of meditation start to reveal themselves more readily to you.

When I began meditating, I found that my quality of sleep improved significantly. As a result, I needed less sleep. My stress levels subsided and my concentration levels improved, as did my memory. My brain just seemed sharper and clearer during the day. Importantly, my dreams became more prolific and I started dreaming in colour, which I had never experienced before. During some of my more profound dreams, I would waken briefly, feeling the need to interpret the significance of my dream and to write it down.

Interestingly, after extensive meditation practice, something in our complexion changes that can catch the attention of others. It's hard to live an unhealthy life when you're meditating regularly. I think people subconsciously tune into those who not only look physically healthy, but whose eyes and face also exude a deep-seated peace. This is most likely because our exterior starts to reflect what's going on in our interior. As they say, the eyes are the windows to the soul.

For those of us who find ourselves quickly at ease with meditating, and do so regularly with great discipline, we may come across more 'higher frequency experiences'. Sensitive people in particular might be able to tune in and see, hear or feel things that are not physically present. Don't be alarmed by these occurrences; just observe them and let them be. If you must, entertain them. You will never be exposed to anything untoward, or to more than that with which you can cope; so there's no need to fear anything during your meditations.

For those who love the experience, there is the option to experiment with additional techniques. By visualising the inhaling and exhaling of different colours – including the inhaling of the future and the exhaling of the past – you can take your meditation to new heights.

If you can tap into the universal force, or prana, through some strong breathing techniques, you can put this energy to good use on your chakras. The chakras comprise seven pairs of energy centres on the front and back of your body. They lie in a straight line, at intervals from one another, from the top of your head down to your pelvic area. If you are sufficiently sensitised, you will feel these spinning vortices or wheels of energy – or at least some of them in the early stages. You might want to read up a little on the Hindu chakra system before discovering your own system. The chakras are extremely useful to work with, not only for your own personal healing, but also for your own spiritual growth. Please don't waste your time wondering whether or not your chakras exist – they're real – so I suggest that for starters, you try to find just one or two of these energy systems on your own body.

I have two final thoughts to share on meditation:

1. There is *no right or wrong way* to meditate. It is just an experience, and hopefully a meaningful one for you.
2. Ensure that you have *no expectations* from your meditation. If you desperately anticipate a particular outcome, it's not going to happen. This is because your thoughts will be hooked into that outcome when you should be completely removing every last thought from your ordinary mind.

> *Meditation is the undisputed pathway to finding peace, happiness and health in body, mind and spirit.*

Meditation is an extremely agile way of freely addressing our wellbeing. If you have not yet experienced the benefits of successful meditation, you are missing out on one of life's greatest gifts.

Much of our Western education encourages us to constantly look outside of ourselves to find the answers for, and comforts to, life's challenges. But for much of the time, we've been looking in the wrong place. Some answers do lie out there, but most of them lie right inside of us all.

Behind the veil

I consider myself extremely fortunate to have made contact with some very spiritually evolved people in my life. Despite the number of charlatans out there, I can guarantee the veracity of the information that I am about to share with you, as it is based on my own first-hand experience. I therefore urge you to keep an open mind, as a frozen mind prevents us from learning the finest of insights that life has to offer.

Psychic Stuart Lawson was the most authentically gifted individual with whom I have ever had the privilege of sitting. In informal terms, he was a clairvoyant, clairaudient and clairsentient, all rolled into one. In other words, he had the ability to see, hear and feel occurrences in the metaphysical world. This included feeling the presence of people who were not physically in the room with him, namely those who had 'crossed over'. He was super-talented and considered the best of his kind in South Africa.

My interaction with Stuart was a turning point for me. He helped me to develop a far greater awareness of this life. He gave me a glimpse into what lies just behind the thin veil of perception (or consciousness) that separates us from a much greater reality beyond what we can physically see, hear, touch and smell.

I first sat with Stuart, who was in his 70s then, after booking my 'reading' with him eight months in advance. Not only was he that sought after, but he saw only four people a day: two in the morning and two in the afternoon.

I had hardly sat down in my chair when Stuart immediately proceeded to tell me, by name in some cases, who had entered the room to join us. At times, he included the finest of details, some of which even I had forgotten. His descriptions of the people, which included their looks, characters and mannerisms, were spot on. Within the first few minutes of my reading, Stuart began talking about my two sons whom he correctly 'saw' as both being alive and well. He then spoke of my daughter. Since I did not have a daughter, I was quick to correct him.

He hesitated and asked me to remain quiet for a while, which I did. He then said that he definitely had my 12-year old little daughter standing next to him in the room. He then stated that my ex-wife had lost this little girl, who would have been born between our two sons. The foetus had naturally aborted at around 10 weeks after conception. According to Stuart, that little girl had come into the room simply to greet me and to send me her love.

I was completely blown away. Only three people had known about the loss of that child from my life: my ex-wife, her gynaecologist and myself. We had chosen not to mention it to family or friends at the time. Back then, we had not known the gender of our unborn child. It was Stuart Lawson who had finally given me clarity on this.

At the end of my hour-long reading, which was packed with life-changing information, I recall just sitting there in front of him, gobsmacked by what he had told me. Everything that he had mentioned was not only accurate, but also relevant and helpful. He had, in an unconventional manner, challenged my conventional thinking. He even predicted some important things in my life that later came to pass.

As you can imagine, I had a million and one questions for him, but I had to leave to make way for the next person who was waiting for their appointment.

Some months later, I sent my father, Neil, who was about 72 years old then, to Stuart Lawson for a reading. It was a gift to my father who was a staunch scientist. While he didn't really buy into any of it, he did trust my sense of healthy intrigue. Just before Neil had agreed to sit with Stuart Lawson, he had fallen ill with cancer. Unfortunately, he died from it some years later. However, by accepting my gift, he had consciously opened his 'curiosity window' for the first time in his life. It allowed a fresh breeze of possibilities to blow in alongside his scientific beliefs.

During Neil's reading, Stuart informed him that an Afrikaner gentleman by the name of Ronnie had joined them in the room. Ronnie had come to thank Neil for helping him just before he had crossed over. Neil was very quick to tell Stuart that, not speaking the language, he had no Afrikaans-speaking friends, and he knew no one by that name.

After some quiet contemplation, Stuart then told Neil that, 40 years previously, he had been a witness to a car accident near to his home at the time (Stuart named the place). He then recounted how he saw Neil stopping at the scene of the accident where a car had crashed into a tree some way from the road.

Behind the steering wheel was a man fighting for his life. Owing to the force of the impact, the man's feet had crumpled up and become stuck under the driver's seat. Neil had managed to free the driver's feet and drag him from the wreckage. An ambulance had later arrived to take the critically injured man to hospital.

Neil was completely flummoxed. How could Stuart Lawson have ever known about that incident, and in such detail? He, himself had completely forgotten about the incident until Stuart Lawson had reminded him of it. Neil also recalled seeing a death notice a few days after the accident in the local newspaper, which had connected the deceased man to the accident site. After 40 years, Neil could not recall the man's actual name, but he did remember that the gentleman had had an Afrikaans surname. My father had never bothered to mention the story to either me or my siblings because it had happened so long ago, before most of us were even born.

❦

I have not the slightest interest in trying to persuade you to go for a reading with a psychic; but I do wish to draw your attention to the fact that there's more to life than meets the eye. There are worlds beyond this one that can be accessed through the practice of stilling one's mind, largely via the art of meditation.

My experiences with Stuart Lawson shifted my thinking so substantially that they provided me with the following insights:

Firstly, after my own sitting, I decided to consult with many spiritually talented individuals, and have continued to do so for more than 20 years. I am completely satisfied that there are people out there who are capable of tapping into an alternative reality. Just because we can't do it, doesn't mean that others can't and that it's all a hoax.

The following analogy may be helpful: we listen to radios, watch TV, use computers and talk on our cellphones on a daily basis. Just because we can't see the radio waves, TV waves, internet waves and cellphone waves that carry our messages through the air does not mean that they don't exist. Of course they do! It is no different with psychics who are able to 'tune into' other frequencies that enable them to hear, see and feel – even smell – a whole host of things that are not normally perceptible to others.

Secondly, owing to the irrefutable evidence offered by Stuart Lawson to both my father and me, I am led to one certain conclusion: there is continuity of life after death. When I write this, I am reminded of that wonderful adage: 'Sleep is a little death, just as death is a little sleep." I'm not for one minute suggesting that I know how it all works, and where we go when we die, but it's very reassuring to know that death is a means to another world, or another reality – just as a car is a means by which to get from point A to point B.

I used to think that it was a tragedy that after enduring, learning and progressing so much over a whole lifetime, at the end of it all, we were simply ashes in the ground. It didn't seem a fitting ending to life, and it all seemed a bit pointless. Now that I know differently, I have tremendous hope. What's more, if we do end up coming back again to live other lives here on Earth – and don't underestimate the support base for reincarnation, especially in the East – then we will need to take a much longer-term view of life here on Earth.

Sir David Attenborough tries desperately to tell us all in his latest SOS to mankind movie *"A Life on Our Planet"* that the destruction of our planet is nearing a point of no return. We can't afford to steer Spaceship Earth on to the (Asteroid) rocks. It would be an extremely bad investment in our own long-term future.

It took one sitting with a spiritually evolved person, combined with some meditation, for me to feel a lot closer to my divinity and the grander scheme of things than I ever had in 11 years of attending church. This is not a criticism of religion, the denomination to which I belonged, or the concept of being a devout churchgoer. My witness statement is that, in taking a more spiritual or mystical approach to this life, I started to get a glimpse of the real me. There's a lot of work ahead, but it has added a whole new dimension to my life.

This much has become clear to me: it is for very good reason that the great spiritual gurus, healers and mystics who walked this Earth all advised us to go within to get closer to the Truth.

Our one and only certainty

There used to be two certainties in our lives: death and taxes.

However, too many people these days consider it a national sport to duck and dive paying their taxes. As a result, tax-paying is no longer a certainty for everyone.

That leaves our own death as the single remaining certainty of which we can all be assured in our lifetimes.

Despite this, most people, in the West in particular, find death too awkward a topic to think about, let alone talk about. Many Westerners actually fear death – some to the point of being thanatophobic.

<୧୨୭୦୨୭>

I had a friend who was a nursing sister. One of her patients had died in his hospital bed while she was on duty. She and a colleague were required to wheel the corpse to the hospital morgue. On their arrival, they had to physically transfer the cadaver from the bed to the morgue table. My friend grasped the man around his upper torso and her colleague placed her arms around his legs. Together they heaved him on to the adjacent table, but as they did that, the man suddenly grunted loudly.

As you can imagine, the two of them shrieked and skedaddled down the corridor, not daring to look back! Soon afterwards, my friend gingerly led a phalanx of doctors back to the morgue to see for themselves whether the miracle man had indeed come back from the dead. Alas, he was as dead as a dodo.

The doctors determined that the nursing sister, while grabbing the upper torso of the corpse, had inadvertently squeezed the remaining air out of the man's lungs. The air had then travelled up through his airways and out over his vocal chords, producing the grunt from the grave.

⊰⋄⊱

My friend can be excused for being 'scared to death' on that occasion. Our English culture, and its language, make no effort to assuage our fears of death either. Does not the image of the Grim Reaper also conjure up unattractive thoughts about death?

I, too, had a memorable lesson on how awkward the topic of death can sometimes be.

⊰⋄⊱

Aeons ago, while I was selling training videos, I found myself calling on a coffin-manufacturing company to try to sell my products. After being introduced to the managing director (MD) of the company, I sat down with him and asked him how his business was going. He responded in a serious tone that his funeral business was alive and well, and that he was busy burying his competition alive.

I didn't know whether to laugh or cry. Instead I tried not to flinch, and continued the conversation as if nothing untoward had been said. When the MD started giggling uncontrollably,

I realised that he had been pulling my leg. I laughed hard, and with some relief, I might add. He confessed that he had been asked that question so often that he had eventually found just the right answer to relax newcomers to his office. He further admitted that he had worked for so long in the business of death that it no longer fazed him one iota.

⋄⋅⋄

I learned two lessons from the coffin factory MD that day. The first was that there is no need to always hold death in such a morbid light. It's a fact of life, and something that we will all have to deal with one day. Secondly, the more familiar you become with something you fear, like death, the less it scares you. That is what encouraged me to personally investigate what death was all about. It did unnerve me back then because I didn't have a clue as to what it was all about.

Stumbling across the works of Dr Elizabeth Kübler-Ross was an enormous find. She's a guru on the subject of loss, grief, near-death experiences and death itself. She has also counselled hundreds – if not thousands – of men, women and children through the process of dying.

In her early work, Kübler-Ross discovered that people who suffer from a significant loss in their lives tend to respond emotionally in a predictably similar way. Whether it's the loss of a relationship, the loss of a job, the loss of one's own business or even the loss of someone close to you, it makes no difference. All losses tend to produce the same five stages of grief in everybody who suffers them.

We would do well to familiarise ourselves with the five stages of grief. They enable us to empathise with others working through serious losses in their own lives. It could also sensitise us to what we might expect to experience when we, too, suffer significant losses in our lives – including the process of losing our own life.

To contextualise the five stages of grief, let's look at Donald Trump's loss (death) of his presidency in the American elections of November 2020. Billions of people witnessed the event unfolding, and even the TV news commentators at the time cited Donald Trump's reaction to the loss of his presidency as mirroring the five stages of grief that are known to precede death.

✧✦✧

When it became clear that Joe Biden had beaten President Donald Trump at the 2020 polls in a nail-biting finish, it came as a shock to President Trump. He refused to acknowledge that he had lost, and instead of congratulating Joe Biden, he went out and played golf for two days. Trump then insisted that electoral fraud had occurred on a massive scale, and continued to insist that he had won the election. He was clearly in *denial* about his loss at the polls.

Some weeks later, the federal courts in America had dismissed all of Trump's 62 electoral fraud challenges, citing insufficient evidence in every case. A highly frustrated Trump retaliated by firing some of his staff, whom he claimed had let him down in the election. In an unprecedented manner, he banned anyone in the White House from assisting Joe Biden's incoming team with the transition of power. Trump had become *angry* at the thought of possibly having to concede power to someone else.

Trump then started *bargaining* with election officials in the states where he had lost, to see if they couldn't perhaps 'find' the required number of votes to overturn the election results in his favour. At a critical stage, Trump tried to leverage what he thought was a bargaining chip by endorsing a mob to overrun Capitol Hill if he was not declared the winner. Trump was actually impeached for endorsing this act of insurrection.

Over the ensuing weeks, Trump hardly spoke to the nation,

and avoided all interaction with the "lamestream media", as he called them. Those who had caught sight of Trump said he looked a dejected man. On the rare occasions that he did appear on the news channels, his sagging body language confirmed this. Reports came in that he was spending a lot of time alone, behind closed doors. Trump became *depressed* at having to face the inevitable.

On the eve of President-elect Biden's inauguration, a truculent Trump knew that he had been cornered. When Trump announced he would not be attending Biden's swearing-in ceremony, the writing was on the wall. He had finally, if not unsportingly, *accepted* defeat.

⋘·⋙

The five identified stages of grief are:[18]

1. Denial
2. Anger
3. Bargaining
4. Depression
5. Acceptance.

These five stages are likely to be exactly what we can expect when we, too, are in the process of facing serious loss, including the loss of our own lives.

Caregivers are all too familiar with how patients react when told that they have terminal cancer. *Denial* strikes when patients simply do not want to believe what the doctor has told them. Many of them go for three – sometimes more – medical opinions in the hope of finding a more friendly diagnosis.

---

[18] Kubler-Ross, E. *On Death and Dying*, Scribner, 2011.

When patients finally realise just how sick they are, they can become very *angry*. They can look jealously at others around them, and ask themselves: "Why me? Why this, and why now?" They can even become angry with themselves and self-flagellate for not having taken better care of themselves.

In trying to *bargain* for one more chance at life, many turn to God and promise to make big changes in their lives if God will just give them one more chance.

When this fails, *depression* sets in, especially when the chemotherapy bites deep. Many negative thoughts can swamp their minds, with regret often topping their list of "if-onlys".

When the person finally *accepts* their fate, their whole demeanour changes and they become calmer. In this final phase, they start saying their goodbyes and preparing for their transition. They get great clarity on what is, and what is not, important in life. For this reason, the dying are among the finest teachers we can encounter.

Now for some more cheerful news: there is a more arm's length approach to the subject of death that we could consider investigating first. It introduces the subject of meeting our Maker a little more gently. I took this route by reading what other people had written about their own near-death experiences (NDEs). An NDE is simply a close encounter with death by someone who was actually in the process of dying, but managed to avoid it at the last minute for some or other reason beyond their conscious control.

My first exposure to NDEs came via a book called *Saved by the Light*[19]. The author, Dannion Brinkley, gave a fascinating

---

[19] Brinkley, D, Perry, P. *Saved by the Light*, HarperTouch, 1995.

account of his own near-death experience after being struck by lightning while talking on his landline. This true story dramatically recounts the events that led to his technically 'dying' several times before the paramedic team was able to repeatedly resuscitate him on the way to the hospital. After fully recovering from his ordeal, he recounted what happened to him when he 'died' – where he went, who he met, who he spoke to, what he saw, and what insights he gained from the whole experience.

A near-death experience completely transforms the lives of those who have them. These people are driven to immediately revisit and re-order their life priorities. Understandably, their interest in the afterlife intensifies, while any fear of death they might have had fades away. Their chase for material wealth is largely abandoned, and their quest to connect to a more spiritual dimension in their lives often becomes their newfound focus. Their deep concern for the welfare of others comes strongly to the fore, often accompanied by their desire to love others unconditionally. These people certainly do go through a profound shift, which is usually irreversible.

Since very few people end up having NDEs, most of us are personally unable to get this first-hand experience of what it might be like to die.

Dr Kübler-Ross, as a scientist, has committed her entire life to studying the process of dying. She has investigated hundreds of NDEs to understand what actually happens to these people when they 'die'. Kübler-Ross is adamant that everyone she interviewed about their NDE essentially said the same thing. For her, it's a knowing, a foregone conclusion that she no longer doubts or questions. What follows are the four phases that

Kübler-Ross maintains we will all experience when we 'cross over'.[20]

The *first phase* is when we experience ourselves 'floating out above our body', like a butterfly emerging from its cocoon. Our senses are all operational, and our 'aerial view' (remember Chapter 1) enables us to see things that we could not see before. Those who were blind can now see; those who suffered paralysis can now walk. All senses are normalised and heightened in this state of being.

The *second phase* is when our dominant guide meets us and introduces us to any other guides who may have been watching over us during our lifetime. If we have never recognised that our 'guides' are with us at all times during our lives, it is now that we discover this truth. For this reason, we are apparently never alone when we die. In this phase, we are also able to go anywhere at the speed of thought. As a result, 'visiting' our earthbound loved ones, wherever they may be, is a matter of applying our minds.

The *third phase* is the transition phase, in which we find ourselves in beautiful, natural surroundings. The location in which we find ourselves symbolises a divide that we need to cross, like a bridge over a lovely river, or a picturesque mountain pass that separates two places, or even a tunnel that joins two places. We are aware of being in the presence of a magnificent light that is not blinding, but splendidly radiant. As this light brightens, it becomes mesmerising, and we feel a deep sense of trust, acceptance and unconditional love in its presence. There's an anticipation of finally 'going home'.

---

20 Kubler-Ross, E. *On Life After Death*, Celestial Arts,1991.

The *fourth phase* is when we are completely enveloped by, and at one with, this light. It overwhelmingly conveys the oneness of everything around us. We realise that this is the Source, the Creator of all consciousness, past, present and future. We just cannot find the words to do justice to this enlightenment we experience. We then confront the totality of our lives in a type of life review. We are made to understand the reasoning behind every thought, word and deed that we ever had in our lives, and the impact that it had on others around us. We understand the concept of free will; the choices we made; whether those choices were our highest choices possible; and whether they made a meaningful difference in the lives of others.

In this final phase, people having an NDE recognise that it's not their time to cross over, so they return to their physical bodies on Earth. Many NDE'ers say that coming back to Mother Earth is a bit of a let-down. This leads one to believe, quite convincingly, which place is Heaven and which one is Hell – if we had to categorise them.

I have no doubt that this is what we'll most likely experience when we die. It certainly sounds like nothing to be afraid of – if anything, quite the opposite.

While people might find Kübler-Ross's research somewhat reassuring, it still requires a leap of faith, and it is a big adjustment from our own thinking. However, it is really important for our own personal growth and spiritual development that we come to terms with our one and only certainty as soon as possible.

The Tibetans are masters at understanding and managing the process of their own people dying. Sogyal Rinpoche, in his *Tibetan Book of Living and Dying* [21] maintains: *"In order to die well, we need to have lived well."*

---

21 Rinpoche, S. *Tibetan Book of Living and Dying*, HarperCollins, 1992.

But what does it really mean to have lived well?

When we get to the finishing line of our lives, we don't want any unfinished business with anyone. We want no lingering regrets about the things we did, or did not do; or for the things we said, or did not say. We don't want anything to reveal that we did not live this life to the full. Neither do we want to be in a position where we only start appreciating what we've got the moment we're about to lose it all. The sooner we show gratitude for what we have in our lives, the better.

To have loved unconditionally and to our heart's content, and to have made a significant difference in the lives of others, is what we might well want our final thoughts to be. Then, say the Tibetans, our death will be a most comforting transition to the afterlife – a fitting climax to a life well lived.

Enlightened leadership

A very greedy form of capitalism is sweeping across our planet today. The chase for material wealth is leaving an enormous spiritual void in its wake. Inequality and poverty for billions of people is inevitable if the Earth's riches are to remain concentrated in fewer and fewer hands. It is going to require extraordinary citizenry, more specifically, extraordinary leadership, to get us out of the planetary mess we're in.

I would, therefore, like to finish both this chapter and this book on a topic close to my heart: leadership. Let this be my clarion call to the up-and-coming generation of leaders: urgently choose a far more enlightened path than your predecessors. Our future leaders need to substantially raise their levels of consciousness if they are to extricate us from the seriousness of the situation in which we find ourselves.

Albert Einstein, who was clearly not just a scientist, said: *"Our problems will no longer be solvable at the same level of consciousness at which they were created."*

One might immediately ask, but who are the exemplars from which the future generations and their leadership can draw their inspiration? Based on currrent performance, it should certainly not be from the world's politicians or businessmen. I am left to conclude that the future generation could start drawing inspiration from the well of wisdom that contains some of the greatest minds that ever walked this planet.

The right 'thought leadership' is available in abundance through the likes of Lao Tzu, the Chinese sage; Confucius, the Chinese moralist; Gautama Buddha, the Hindu avatar; Socrates, the Greek philosopher; Omar Khayyam, the Sufi mystic; Dogen, the Zen Buddhist monk; Black Elk, the Native American visionary; Sathya Sai Baba, the Hindu guru and philanthropist; and Albert Einstein, the scientist and philosopher.

There are many more such minds from which to draw. Some iconic exemplars from the modern era include the likes of Martin Luther King, Mahatma Gandhi, Nelson Mandela and the Dalai Lama – all of whom are spiritual statesmen rather than smarmy politicians.

⋘•⋙

You can imagine my elation when I met Nelson Mandela in the flesh. Madiba, as he was affectionately called, had, in the dying moments of apartheid, rescued our country from civil war. He had paid the hefty price of serving 27 years in jail before finally bringing the Nationalist Party and its abhorrent racist policies to its knees.

Our serendipitous meeting happened in Exclusive Books. I was alone, browsing the 'Spiritual' section, and Madiba had slipped into the shop quietly with his bodyguard. The door had immediately been locked behind them both to prevent the gathering crowds from swamping the shop. It was quite a surreal moment because there I was, standing with one of the most evolved people of our time – and I had him all to myself! Madiba's engaging demeanour was one of his most endearing characteristics. That afternoon, he was particularly interested in my life, including the book that I was buying. What a fateful coincidence it was for me to show him a copy of *The Golden Key to Happiness*[22], which I was buying.

That most fortuitous encounter with Madiba motivated me to better understand what drove prodigious leaders like him; the qualities they possessed; and why they were so admired by hundreds of millions of people around the globe. So, after many years of listening to, reading about, observing, meeting and experiencing the character traits of extraordinarily gifted trailblazers in all walks of life, I have come to the following conclusions about the kind of leadership that I believe the world is in desperate need of today.

<∰⋅∰>

Essential characteristics of enlightened leadership

Enlightened leaders exude a deep sense of moral rectitude. They have a passionate concern for the welfare of others, and a spiritual-like purpose behind everything that they say and do. They are wise beyond their years, and possess moral compasses that point permanently to true north. With every step they take, their gravitas portrays the image of a life well lived. Their trademark characteristic is that they treat everyone respectfully,

---

[22] Saionji, M. *The Golden Key to Happiness*, Booksurge, 1995.

regardless of their station in life. Such leaders act consistently in accordance with an impeccable set of values. They distance themselves from any individual or institution that may discredit their reputation. They recognise that reputation is like fitness: it takes forever to get, but it can be lost very quickly. They appreciate that anything worth having takes time to accumulate, and must therefore be nurtured and protected.

In the volatile, uncertain, complex and ambiguous world in which we live, the wise seem comfortable with the impermanence of everything around them. In their minds, nothing lasts forever and everything is in constant renewal. Therefore, letting go, or detaching themselves from things, is second nature to them – because creating expectations via attachment is a sure-fire way of being disappointed. They simply let it go, and let it be.

They prioritise simplicity in their lives. Unlike most others, they don't spend the first 40 years of their lives tying a whole lot of knots; and then the next 40 years undoing them all. They may have an appreciation for the complicated, but are able to package the complex in simple terms. Less is more to them. There are no hidden agendas with such leaders – what you see is what you get. They are usually candid individuals with high levels of transparency in what they think, say and do.

All of the exemplars of leadership that I proposed earlier were highly introspective about life itself. They spent many hours alone, in silence, exploring the inner realms of their minds. As a result, they came up with extraordinary solutions to complex problems. In short, they were disciplined meditators. This is known of the Dalai Lama, who is a practising Buddhist; but it is not commonly known that Nelson Mandela meditated every day in his prison cell. I am personally convinced that this was the major source of his wisdom, which he shared with the world in his halcyon days.

These people are the givers, not the takers in this life. They are all too familiar with the joy that can be found by giving unconditionally to others. They are at ease with this, knowing full well that the universe has an uncanny way of returning generosity with interest. That is why they never deny others the pleasure of giving to them.

Enlightened leaders are the warriors – not the worriers – of this life. They are fearless in seeking to better understand themselves and others along the road. They are like that blade of grass that bends in the wind, but can crack cement when it needs to. They see the futility in worry, because 99% of what they worry about never actually materialises.

They are eternal students of this life, and their humility in this regard is palpable. This makes for a very refreshing contrast to the tyranny of the ego that dominates much of the political and commercial leadership today.

These leaders have an intuitive understanding about matters of life that is hard to fathom; but it clearly separates them from others. They are able to get to the root cause of things via an acute insight that is not easily found in others. They are philosophers of note, and are therefore the living archetypes of Socrates' maxim: *"The unexamined life is not worth living."*

Leaders of this ilk demonstrate advanced levels of emotional competence. They are conciliatory and non-judgmental, rarely finding the need to criticise others. They appreciate that it's not really what you say, but how you say it – and even more importantly, when you say it, because timing is everything. They go long-term in everything that they do, and they practise plenty of patience and delayed gratification along the way. These leaders are unflappable, exuding calm in the presence of others. Amid the noise and haste of modern life, their serenity is heartfelt and disarming. They have a lightness of being about them.

These informed leaders are astute and interested listeners, and often the last to speak. When they finally speak up, everyone tends to listen, as they have earned their right to speak. They tend not to talk about themselves, but instead show a keen interest in others.

Finally, and importantly in the context of this book, these wise people have a balanced, but prioritised, approach to life. They have the foresight to take care of their health first. They know full well that without a healthy mind, body and spirit, it is not feasible to climb the ladder towards anything more meaningful in this life.

I'm not suggesting for one minute that these people walk on water; nor do I recall them ever publicly professing to have any extraordinary spiritual powers. But they do aspire to high ideals.

We are in dire need of high-calibre citizens in leadership positions across all walks of society today - especially in my own home country! The future is bristling with change, and we need modern leaders that can embrace this challenge.

So, don your spiritual armour, and as Mahatma Gandhi so fittingly said: *"Be the change that you wish to see in the world."*

And remember: this change starts with you.

I wish you well on your journey.

READING LIST

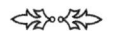

Albom, Mitch: *Tuesdays with Morrie* (1997)
Albom, Mitch: *The First Call from Heaven* (2013)
Albom, Mitch: *Five People You Meet in Heaven* (2003)
Arbesman, Samuel: *The Half-life of Facts* (2004)
Branson, Richard: *Like A Virgin* (2012)
Brennan, Barbara: *Hands of Light* (1988)
Brennan, Barbara: *Light Emerging* (1993)
Brinkley, Dannion: *Saved by the Light* (1994)
Buckland, Raymond: *Doors to Other Worlds* (1994)
Buscaglia, Leo: *Born for Love* (1992)
Carlson,: Richard: *Don't Sweat the Small Stuff* (1997)
Carnegie, Dale: *How to Win Friends and Influence People* (1965)
Carnegie, Dale: *How to Stop Worrying and Start Living* (1956)
Chopra, Deepak: *The Path to Love* (1997)
Chopra, Deepak: *The Seven Spiritual Laws of Success* (1996)
Chopra, Deepak: *Perfect Health* (1990)
Chopra, Deepak: *Quantum Healing* (1989)
Ciaramicoli, Arthur: *The Power of Empathy* (2000)
Coleman, Vernon: *Overcoming Stress* (1995)
Collins, Jim: *Good to Great* (2001)
Collins, Mabel: *Light on the Path: Through the Gates of Gold* (1997)
Collins, Bryn: *Emotional Unavailability* (1997)
Covey, Stephen: *The Seven Habits of Highly Effective People* (1994)
de Bono, Edward: *Simplicity* (1998)
Dyer, Wayne: *Real Magic – Creating Miracles in Everyday Life* (1993)
Fontana, David: *The Elements of Meditation* (1994)
Forward, Susan: *Toxic Parents* (1990)
Freke & Gandy, Timothy & Peter: *World Mysticism* (1997)
Gates, Bill: *The Road Ahead* (1995)
Gladwell, Malcolm: *Outliers* (2008)
Gladwell, Malcolm: *What the Dog Saw* (2009)
Gladwell, Malcolm: *The Tipping Point* (2000)
Goleman, Daniel: *Social Intelligence* (2006)
Goleman, Daniel: *Emotional Intelligence* (1996)
Gray, John: *Men are from Mars, Women are from Venus* (1993)
Griscom, Chris: *The Healing of Emotion* (1988)
Griscom, Chris: *Ecstasy is a New Frequency* (1987)
Hall, Doriel: *Healing with Meditation* (1996)

Hauck, Paul: *How to Love and be Loved* (1997)
Hey, Louise: *You can Heal your Life* (1984)
Hill, Napoleon: *Think and Grow Rich* (1988)
Holbeche, Soozi: *Awakening to Change* (1993)
Holbeche, Soozi: *The Power of Gems and Crystals* (1989)
Holbeche, Soozi: *The Power of Your Dreams* (1992)
Hollis, James: *What Matters Most* (2010)
Hunt, John: *The Art of the Idea* (2009)
Isaacson, Walter: *Steve Jobs* (2011)
Johnson, Boris: *The Churchill Factor* (2015)
Johnson, Lee: *How to Escape Your Comfort Zones* (1995)
Judith, Anodea: *Eastern Body, Western Mind* (2004)
Karagulla & van Gelder, Shafica & Dora: *The Chakras and the Human Energy Fields* (1994)
Kehoe, John: *A Vision of Power and Glory* (1994)
Kingma, Daphne: *The 9 Types of Love* (1999)
Kiyosaki, Robert: *Rich Dad's Guide to Investing* (1998)
Kotter, John: *Leading Change* (1996)
Kubler-Ross, Elizabeth: *On Life After Death* (1991)
Kubler-Ross, Elizabeth: *The Wheel of Life* (1999)
Kubler-Ross, Elizabeth: *Life Lessons* (2000)
Lama, Dalai: *Ancient Wisdom, Modern World* (1999)
Lama, Dalai: *The Art of Happiness* (1998)
Linn, Denise: *Past Lives, Present Dreams* (1994)
Lorie & Mascetti, Peter & Manuela: *The Quotable Spirit* (1996)
MacLaine, Shirley: *Out on a Limb* (1983)
Mandela, Nelson: *Long Walk to Freedom* (1994)
Mandino, Og: *University of Success* (1983)
Maxwell, John: *15 Invaluable Laws of Growth* (2012)
McCormack, Mark: *What they Don't Teach You at Harvard Business School* (1984)
McQueen, Michael: *Winning the Battle for Relevance* (2013)
Moore, Thomas: *Soul Mates* (1994)
Mouton, Jannie: *And then they fired me* (2011)
Myss, Caroline: *Anatomy of Spirit* (1996)
Myss, Caroline: *The Creation of Health* (1993)
Nairn, Rob: *Living, Dreaming, Dying* (2002)
Newton, Michael: *Journey of Souls* (1994)

Peck, Scott: *Further Along the Road Less Travelled* (1993)
Pretorius, Brand: *In the Driving Seat* (2013)
Rabbin, Robert: *The Sacred Hub* (1996)
Ramacharaka, Yogi: *The Hindu-Yogi Science of Breath* (1960)
Rampa, Lobsang: *The Third Eye* (1995)
Reibstein, Janet: *Love Life* (1997)
Rendel, Peter: *Understanding the Chakras* (1990)
Rinpoche, Sogyal: *The Tibetan Book of Living and Dying* (1992)
Robert, Michael: *The New Strategic Thinking* (2006)
Ruskan, John: *Emotional Clearing* (1993)
Saionji, Masami: *The Golden Key to Happiness* (1995)
Sandberg, Sheryl: *Lean In* (2013)
Schroeder, Alice: *The Snowball* (2009)
Schwartz, David: *The Magic of Thinking Big* (1987)
Sharma, Robin: *The Monk Who Sold his Ferrari* (1997)
Sherwood, Keith: *The Art of Spiritual Healing* (1994)
Smith, Gerard: *Celebrating Success* (1997)
Stein, Diane: *Essential Reiki* (1995)
Steiner, Claude: *Emotional Literacy* (1997)
Tolle, Eckhart: *The Power of Now* (1999)
Van der Merwe, Merwede: *Meditation: A Path to Consciousness* (1997)
Vance, Ashlee: *Elon Musk* (2015)
Walsch, Neale: *Conversations with God: Books 1, 2 and 3* (1998)
Wauters, Ambika: *Journey of Self Discovery* (1996)
Weiss, Brian: *Many Lives, Many Masters* (1996)
Weiss, Brian: *Messages from the Masters* (2000)
West-Meads, Zelda: *The Trouble with You* (1995)
Williamson, Linda: *Contacting the Spirit World* (1996)
Wimala, Bhante: *Lesson of the Lotus* (1997)
Yu, Dan: *Confucius from the Heart* (2006)
Zukav, Gary: *The Seat of the Soul* (1990)
Zukav, Gary: *Soul Stories* (2000)

Printed in Great Britain
by Amazon